GARY JOBSON'S
How to Sail

Foreword by TED TURNER

Illustrations by JOHN MECRAY

GARY JOBSON'S
How to Sail

Foreword by Ted Turner
Illustrations by John Mecray

ZIFF-DAVIS BOOKS
NEW YORK

*To my parents
and my wife, Janice.*

First Printing, 1980.

Library of Congress Catalog Card Number: 80-81035
ISBN: 0-87165-061-4 (hardcover); 0-87165-064-9 (paperback)

Design: Virginia Tiso Gianakos

Ziff-Davis Publishing Company
One Park Avenue
New York, N.Y. 10016

ACKNOWLEDGMENTS

I would like to thank the following for their aid and assistance, advice and encouragement: Charles E. Kanter of Pasadena, Maryland for his contributions to the catamaran section; Karina Paape, my trusted associate in Annapolis for much of the research and push to finish the book; Mark Robinson of West Coast Water Sports, Inc. of Clearwater, Florida for his guidance on windsurfing; Eric Skemp of AMF/Alcort for his many contributions and ideas; and Tony Meisel, my trusted editor at Ziff-Davis Books for his brushing on the final strokes of this book and many of the ideas contained herein.

Thanks also to John Martin, Tad LaFountain, Sam Merrick, Joe Prosser, Don Cohan, Dick Curry, Chuck Inglefield, Timmy Larr, Dick Lamb, Joe O'Hora, Michael Crowley, Steve Baker, Ted Turner and all the great people I've had the opportunity to sail with over the years . . . they've contributed a lot!

CONTENTS

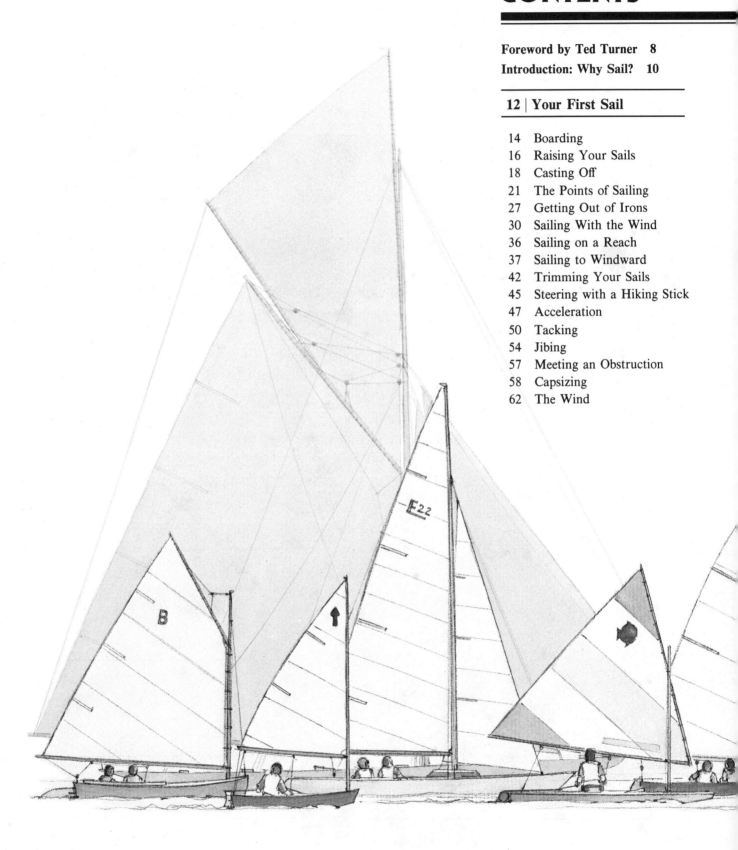

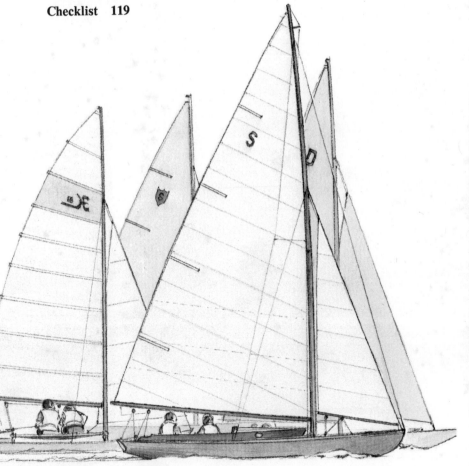

FOREWORD

You've bought *How to Sail* because you've just got your first boat, or are thinking of taking the plunge. There's no sport I know more relaxing than sailing. Or competitive. Or exhilarating. It appeals to putterers, demons and just plain folk. You can do it for as long as you can move, and you can sail anywhere in the world, except maybe the middle of a desert.

Sure, you can learn to sail at a school or by trial and error, but with a copy of *How to Sail* in hand, you'll be able to teach yourself, and save a couple of bucks to boot. Gary will show you all the techniques: tacking, jibing, boat handling, seamanship, ropes and knots, the works. But he'll also give you confidence, and there's nothing that makes for a better sailor. The water can be scary first time out. Gary's book will help you get over your fears and get you sailing well enough to cope with whatever comes along. And as you sail more and more, your faith in your own ability will increase, you'll become more daring and you'll get better and better. You'll find a new kind of freedom and self-assuredness. It's a new life and a renewal of life itself.

I first met Gary Jobson in 1972, at the Solo Regatta in Barrington, Rhode Island. I came in seventh, and here was this kid, still in school, who cleaned up. It wasn't luck. He knew all the moves —tactical, psychological and technical. He played wind and waves with the finesse of an old pro and outguessed a lot of international class sailors. He was damn good!

Well, he's still good . . . so good, in fact, that I don't go sailing in any major competition without him as my tactician and right-hand man. Gary is a sailor's sailor, and a sharp-thinking one at that.

Over the years we've sailed thousands of miles together, all over the world, in every conceivable set of conditions. He's never failed me or the rest of the crew in getting the most out of every boat, every contest. In the tragic Fastnet Race of 1979, he steered *Tenacious* in 20- to 30-foot seas for over four hours without a broach. Truly a remarkable feat!

But as great a sailor as Gary is, he's a better teacher and coach. He has the knack of making theory effortless and practice fun. I've watched him working with sailors of all levels of skill, from kids in optimist prams to yacht club heavies tucked into the cockpits of their IOR machines. He's clear, level-headed, patient and never condescending.

How to Sail will open up a new world. And unlike some other books I've read, it won't bog you down with outworn concepts, useless information or dull theory. Gary literally takes you sailing, from the moment you step on board 'til you arrive safely back at the dock. The book embodies his great technical skills and his spirit and love of the sport. It makes sailing fun! You can't ask for anything more.

——————————————*Ted Turner*

Introduction
WHY SAIL?

Over 35 million Americans participate in some form of boating every year. Why do people sail? What is it that attracts people to the sea or to lakes?

Sailing covers a full range of activities, offering a niche for almost anyone's level of skill and purse. With so many types of sailing—from cruising to day-sailing, windsurfing to Olympic competition—there's something for everyone.

The primary goal of most sailors has been cruising and day-sailing, though the keenest sailors gravitate to racing, where sailing becomes more serious. Keeping your boat moving faster than the competition creates a special aura for racing.

Unlike many activities in which athletes are washed-up at an early age, sailors can begin to compete as early as age seven and continue their competitive careers well into their sixties or older. Three American skippers in the 1972 Olympic games were all in their forties, and each won a medal. There's no such thing as an "over the hill gang" in sailing. Sir Francis Chichester did a single-handed circumnavigation of the globe when he was in his seventies. Once you learn the basics, sailing is exciting, fun, and best of all, easy.

But sailing is more than a sport, it's a life-style. People dress for it, eat by it, travel to it, and socialize with it. Sailing is an excellent family activity because everyone can participate and everyone can contribute.

As the energy crisis becomes more intense, people will take a closer look at sailing. It is an environmentally safe activity that, unlike powerboating, isn't tied to fuel supplies. As our oil wells run dry many powerboat owners will shift to sail. Currently, there are studies under way on the feasibility of sailing ships to transport cargo across the oceans. With the present rise in oil prices this is looking more likely every year.

Sailing has the undeserved reputation of being a rich man's sport. In fact, Commodore Vanderbilt was once asked how much his yacht cost, and replied: "If you have to ask how much it cost, you can't afford it." This is not true today. Sailing is one of the least expensive recreational activities. The cost per hour of sailing ranks among the lowest of all recreational activities.

Used boats trade on an active market at reasonable prices. When you buy a sailboat, you are making an investment, not taking a risk. Of course, the time involved in maintaining a boat can be great, but this too becomes part of the fun.

Spectators don't follow yacht racing as they do sports such as football, basketball, baseball, and tennis. However, public interest in the spectacle of sailing is growing. Over 200,000 people are on the water to watch the America's Cup races, and thousands line the shores of San Francisco Bay to watch maxi ocean-racing yachts sail around the buoys each September. Over two million people will watch the tall ships sail into Boston Harbor in 1980.

You *can* learn to sail in a short time. I once had a student at the U.S. Merchant Marine Academy who had never sailed before. Within three years he had been named to the All-American Collegiate Sailing Team.

The key is setting a goal for yourself, be it day-sailing on a lake or working yourself up to Olympic competition. You'll have something to work for and something to look back on with satisfaction. Unfortunately, many people sail for thirty years without improving themselves. Constantly setting a goal, reaching it, and then setting new goals, will improve your skills in a short time.

Learning to sail is not the mystery so many people think it is. The biggest fear many have is fear of the water and capsizing. But sailing is fun, and part of that fun can be capsizing.

When undertaking a sport or activity for the first time many people take lessons. Be it tennis, skiing, golf, or flying, introductory lessons are offered to get you hooked on the sport. Unfortunately, it is difficult to find a place, and often a way, to take sailing lessons. Many people purchase boats without ever having been on one, coaxed by zealous dealers or ads in magazines. The concept of this book is to give you lessons which will make you feel relaxed and comfortable with sailing.

You can read about "how to sail," but this book will give you the opportunity to find out exactly what it *feels* like to be in a boat, and how to deal emotionally with the problems that arise.

YOUR FIRST SAIL

Let's get ready to go sailing. No need to wait around. Theory and terms will come as we learn. First you need to put the boat in the water. Although there are different techniques for launching, as described later on, it is best to have an experienced sailor with you for the first time.

Relax. Try to stay loose. Sailing is fun and easy. In fact, the first times are often the best; much like a skier going down a slope on his first run.

Once the boat is in the water, secure it to a section of the dock or on a mooring so that the bow is pointing as directly into the wind as possible. It is best to locate the boat on a part of the dock that is easy to maneuver away from, clear of obstacles. Run through the checklist we will develop to be sure that all the necessary equipment is on board.

Keep in mind that many people on the water may be as inexperienced as you, and may be unable to get out of your way. Caution is the rule at all times when sailing.

Boarding

Boarding a sailboat for the first time is an exciting experience for everyone, but it can be traumatic. This is normal. All sailors feel excitement grow as they step on board their yacht. You must be careful when boarding a boat; even experienced sailors have fallen in the water. Always wear non-skid deck shoes to give you better footing, and also to protect the deck. Wearing socks with your shoes will add to your traction. Board your boat quickly and keep your hands clear. To steady yourself, hold onto a shroud or rail while stepping on board, or hold the steadying hand of a person already on the boat. Don't step from dock to deck with an armful of gear. Pass your gear across to the boat first. Step into the boat as close to the middle as you can. On smaller boats it is imperative to step into the middle of the boat while keeping your weight low. It often helps to put the centerboard halfway down while loading the boat to give it added stability. Keep the deck clear by stowing your gear as it is passed onboard. Most importantly, relax when boarding, but don't take unnecessary chances. Falling into the water between boat and dock can be dangerous.

Sit in the most comfortable spot. The helmsman (the person steering) has to sit in a position near the tiller. The helmsman should try to sit so the hiking stick is at a 90 degree angle to the tiller. On a boat with a wheel, it is best to stand while steering. This gives the helmsman a better view of both sails and where he is heading.

Each crew member normally has a specific place to sit when leaving the dock and when under way. Always keep your head down to avoid being hit by the boom. Normally, most of the crew weight is kept at the beamiest (widest) part of the boat.

Run through all the motions of boarding on land first, or on a dock, to get the feeling of the boat in the water.

Now that you are on board, run through your checklist (figure 1). Are the halyards clear and the sails ready to go up? Are the battens in their pockets? Are your sheets uncoiled? It is important that your lines be uncoiled so they do not foul up in a block while you are attempting to leave the dock.

Attach your rudder to the boat and be sure it is in the correct position. Most rudders will use a stop just above the rudder pintle and gudgeon (see figure 2) to prevent the rudder from popping out. Newer boats often have swing rudders which should be secured in the lowered position.

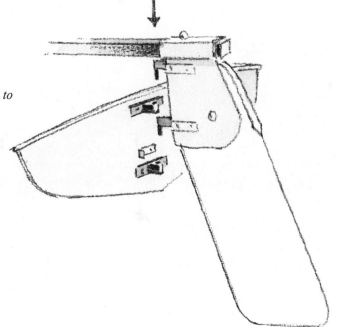

2. Pintles and gudgeons are the simplest way to attach the rudder to the boat.

Raising Your Sails

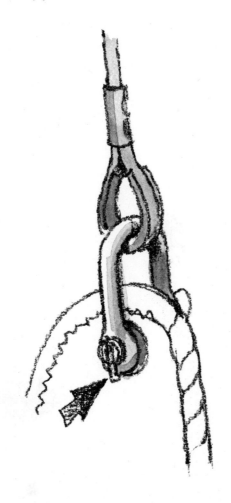

3. Always make sure shackles are securely fastened.

Raise the mainsail first. Check all the shackles to be sure they are secure. Many shackles are of a twist-locking type with a little groove for the pin. Make sure it is in the proper place (see figure 3). Keep just enough slack in the mainsheet so that the sails will fill, but not so much that the mainsheet catches. Keep the mainsheet clear of the winches, cleats, and even the stern of the boat. Stay low so you don't get hit in the head.

While the mainsail is being hauled to the top of the mast, feed the luff of the mainsail (bolt rope) up through the mast slot to keep it from jamming (see figure 4). If you have a sleeve-type sail, be sure the luff of the sail is slid along the mast evenly. Next, haul up the jib. Keep the foot of the jib over the deck so it won't fall in the water. Raise it quickly, so it won't go overboard. As soon as the jib halyard is cleated, prepare to cast off.

Before leaving the dock check once again that all the equipment is stowed. Cleat the halyards using a figure eight followed by a half hitch (see figure 5). On a boat with a winch to assist you in handling the halyard, keep at least four turns of the halyard on the winch. If the halyard is wire, wrap the wire around the winch until the rope tail is clear and cleat the rope (see figure 6).

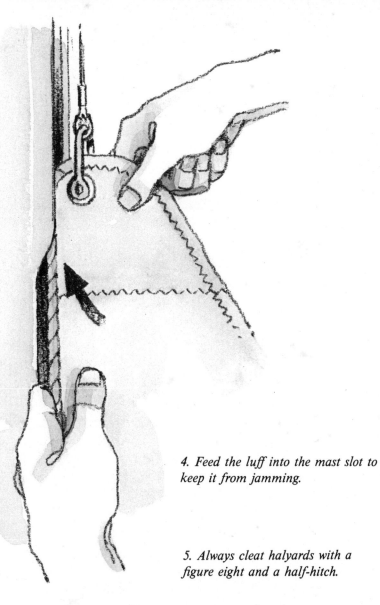

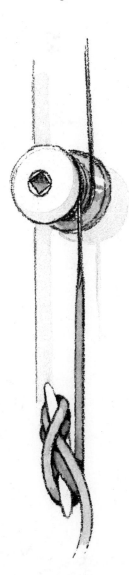

6. *Wire halyards must clear the winch, with the rope tail cleated.*

4. *Feed the luff into the mast slot to keep it from jamming.*

5. *Always cleat halyards with a figure eight and a half-hitch.*

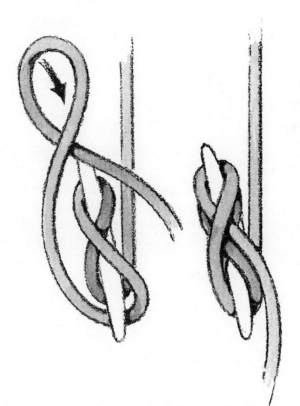

Casting Off

With the sails up and eased out and your rudder in position, put the centerboard all the way down and use the rudder to aim the bow into the wind. Be patient—it often takes time for the boat to swing around. In heavier winds the boat will move back and forth and will be more likely to be unstable. Be patient, stay calm, and keep your weight toward the middle of the boat.

Cast off your painter (bow line) and allow the boat to begin to drift backwards. Keep the crew sitting in their normal position during this time. Remind them to stay low. As the boat gains momentum you will be able to steer it in reverse. Once it begins moving, pull the helm—the tiller— over to one side. If you want to sail on the port tack put the helm on the port side (left) of the boat. If you want to start sailing on the starboard tack put the helm on the starboard side (right) of the boat. Keep the helm to one side so the bow swings away from the wind. When the wind is blowing abeam (across your boat), trim in your sails until they stop luffing. Once you begin trimming sails, the boat will begin to heel to leeward. This is normal, and a regular part of sailing, but can be a little scary to the new sailor.

Sit on the windward side of the boat where you can see both sails working together while watching the approaching wind and waves. Sitting to windward gives you a clear view where you are heading and what is happening in your boat. Keep your back to the wind, face the sail, and sit up on the side of the deck in order to keep the boat flat. If the boat begins to heel excessively (leaning to leeward), ease the main boom out using the mainsheet, and head the boat into the wind by pushing the tiller to leeward (away from you). Both of these actions (with the mainsheet and the tiller) will reduce the force of the wind in your sails.

As you begin trimming your sails, pull the tiller toward you. This will help your boat to steer away from the wind. Normally, filling the sails will force the boat to round back toward the wind. The counteracting force of the rudder and the sails together will help you gain forward momentum.

Your goal is to steer in a straight line. Make a game out of sailing. As the boat begins to sail, pick an object on shore or on the water to head for. Having a target to point the boat towards makes it easy to watch where you go. If it is an object in the water like a buoy (see figure 7), channel marker, or an anchored boat, watch the motion of your reference in relation to the shoreline in the background. It's easy to see if you are altering course inadvertently. Another technique is to watch the wake, or the trail of your waves, coming from the stern of your boat. If you have a straight trail you have been sailing a straight course. However, a snake-like trail tells you that you have not been steering in a straight line. Reaching the object you have been heading for, pick another and start again.

An old saying goes, "Give me a star to steer by and I will be able to steer anywhere." Sailors most enjoy steering. You get the greatest feeling from the boat and also gather a closeness with the wind and waves. The most important person on the boat at any given time is normally the helmsman. The helmsman controls the course and is in a position to see all the action outside as well

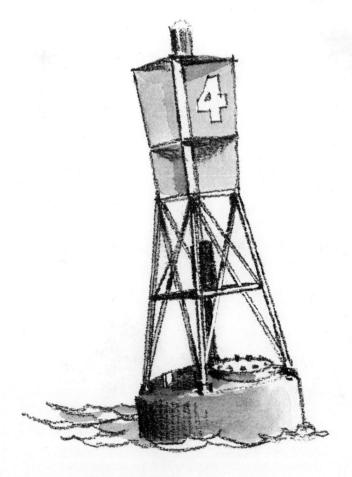

7. *A buoy makes a good mark to steer toward.*

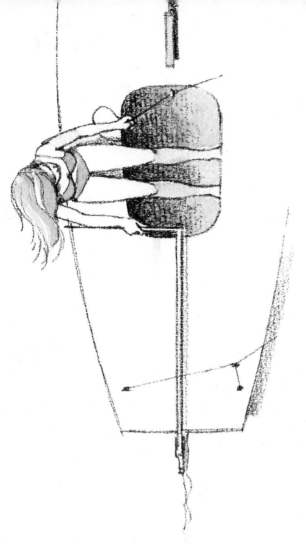

8. Keep your arms and legs parallel.

9. Using a hiking stick and strap.

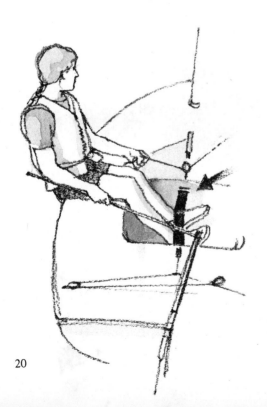

as within the boat. The helmsman is usually the skipper and the person in charge, although this was not always true. On Lord Nelson's boat, *Victory,* it took as many as eight men to handle the four wheels which turned the rudder. In addition, the wheels were under a deck that allowed very little visibility. The watch officer on the deck above called the orders to the helm. In yachting competition in the last century, much of the steering was done by professional sailors, although today the International Yacht Racing Rules do not allow professional sailors to steer during a race.

Hold the mainsheet with your forward hand and the tiller with your aft hand. Crossing your hands causes confusion. Remember, the trick to steering well is to use your body weight, the trim of your sails, and the rudder all together. The combination of all three makes for a good helmsman. Although sailing takes considerable practice and coordination, it is easy to do because each function (weight, sails, and rudder) becomes natural and is interdependent. Staying organized is important in a boat. You will be more comfortable and effective as a crew member or helmsman. Also, distributing your weight evenly on both legs and sitting with good posture will give you greater endurance. The best sailors always seem to look good in a boat. Let's learn the correct way now.

Keep your weight evenly distributed when sitting on the side of the boat with your arms and legs parallel (see figure 8). By keeping your arms parallel to your legs you will be in a better position to maneuver. If you are using a hiking strap to extend your weight over the side (see figure 9), keep your weight equally distributed on both legs. You won't tire as easily and you'll sail better.

A sailboat can only be maneuvered when it is

moving. Sailboats can't maneuver when stopped. The faster a boat is moving the easier it is to turn, much like a car. At low speeds a car is difficult to maneuver, while at high speeds the slightest turn of the wheel will cause it to turn quickly. Try to turn your boat smoothly so you lose little speed during a maneuver. You will find that the faster you turn your boat, the faster it will lose speed. Of course, this can be advantageous if you need to stop quickly, say if you were landing at a dock or a mooring. On the other hand, maneuvering on the water you do not want to lose speed so slower maneuvering is in order.

The Points of Sailing

Sailboats move through the water on three basic courses. Usually they sail fastest on a reach when the wind is hitting the boat from abeam. If the wind is forward of abeam (coming from ahead) we call it close reaching. If the wind is aft of abeam we term it broad reaching. Let's start with reaching because it is the easiest point to sail. The best winds to learn to sail in range between 4 and 10 knots (a knot is one nautical mile per hour). Lighter winds make it difficult to maneuver while heavier winds require greater skill. Light-to-moderate breezes and small waves allow the boat to sail easily without problems. The crew will feel more secure. Pick a course to sail and turn the boat toward where you would like to go. (See figure 10.)

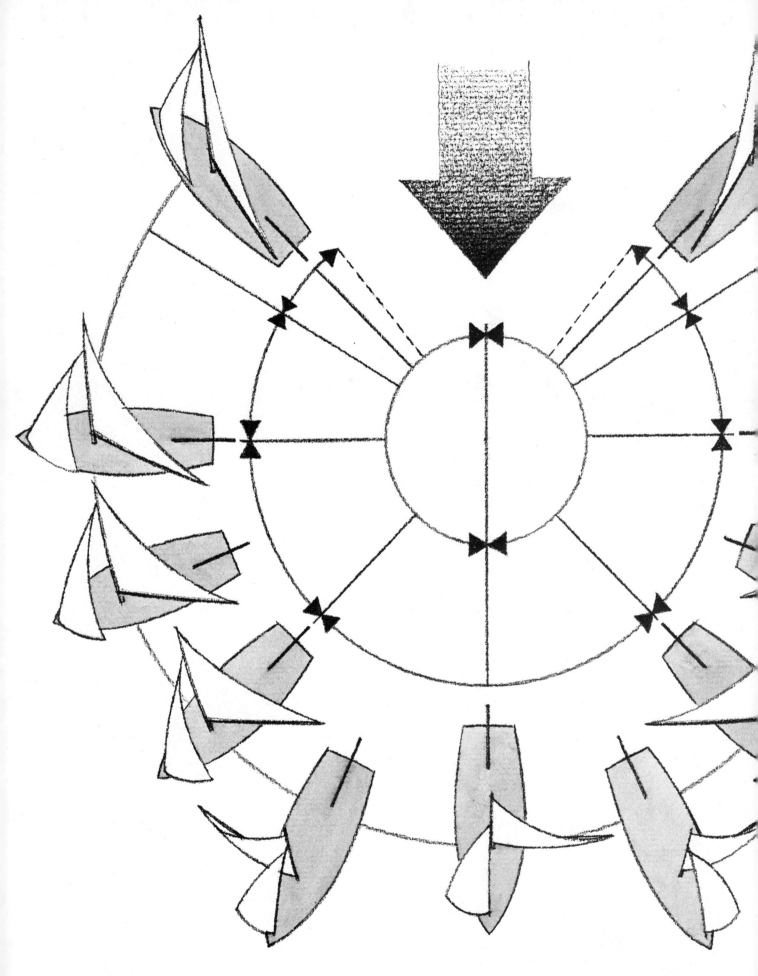

10. The points of sailing. Most boats sail fastest on a beam reach. The diagram shows relative sail trim in relation to wind direction.

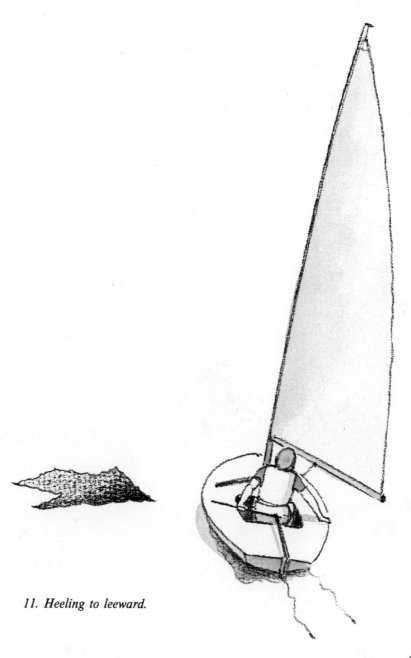

11. Heeling to leeward.

In very light winds (under 6 knots) sit toward the middle of the boat, allowing the boat to heel to leeward slightly. Heeling to leeward helps the sails take shape and the boat to sail on its lines (see figure 11). All boats are designed to sail at a specific angle of heel. Picture for a moment what a boat must look like from under the water. In many ways it resembles a fish. It moves through the water efficiently. Designers try to come up with the best possible hull shape that works on all points of sail. But a boat will sail best on a particular set of lines. Understanding this is told through steering. When sailing, the boat should have a slight bit of windward helm. "Windward helm" are the forces which make the boat luff or round up toward the wind. If the boat heads toward the wind you have windward helm. There are many factors which determine how much windward helm exists. The angle of heel—to what degree the boat is heeling to leeward—is one of the most important. Generally, the greater the leeward heel the more windward helm will be created. By sailing the boat more upright you can reduce the amount of windward helm, or the force rounding you into the wind. A slight windward helm is good and helps you to steer better.

In breezy winds sit on the windward side of the boat to help it stay on an even keel. Normally, most boats sail best when they are upright or have just a slight (5 degrees) leeward heel. The boat will sail more efficiently then. In whatever winds always face the sail. Even many Olympic sailors fail to steer well because they do not keep good posture when sitting in the boat. You won't make these mistakes in the early going if you go out with an experienced sailor. Even in a boat designed for single-handed sailing (one person at a time) taking a second person along will be helpful. You will both fit. Do not worry about capsizing at this point. Capsizing can be a lot of fun, at least in warm weather. Relax and enjoy yourself; think about your course and concentrate on your posture in the boat and how you are steering and playing the sails. Start cautiously and build experience. Try not to be complacent about capsizing, however. Even after twenty years of sailing I am still concerned about capsizing and being able to handle my boat. By following these techniques I have been able to avoid capsizing. Concentration is the key.

Building experience and drawing on the past I have overcome my sailing fears. The same will help you. Since you are new to sailing you may not have past experience to draw from. A helpful trick is to mentally run through every step before you get on the water. You'll feel more relaxed as things actually happen.

Close your eyes and sit back. Picture yourself and the boat on the water. Watch other boats. Keep in mind all the maneuvers you will be making. It may also be helpful to watch boats that are actually sailing on the water. Imagine being in one of the boats. Try to judge what you might do. It's a good technique for developing options and confidence. Follow each step you've thought out, running through them by the numbers.

When leaving the dock, or maneuvering, only one voice should be heard. The helmsman, or skipper, is the person to give the orders. The boat will be better organized and there will be less chance for confusion. The rule of thumb is, "For every additional person you add to a boat you square your problems."

As you begin to sail keep your attention on several areas. First, heed your course and your heading. Second, watch the wind approaching

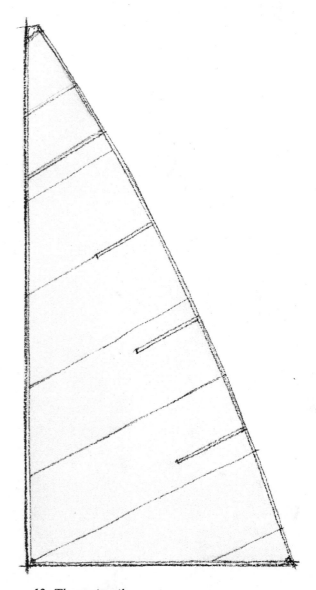

12. The mainsail.

13. When a sail is correctly trimmed
it ceases to luff.

your boat by the ripples on the water and make adjustments to anticipate the increased wind strength. Third, watch your sails to ensure that they are trimmed correctly at all times. Fourth, watch the crew and what they are doing in the boat. You'll have fewer problems in the future. The helmsman is always in the best position to watch what is going on. Every five to ten seconds you should check each of these things. It is much like glancing in the rearview mirror every few seconds when driving.

Develop a checklist in the back of your mind of things to follow. Keep saying to yourself, "How is my course? What is the wind doing now? What is the next set of waves like? How are my sails trimmed? Is the boat organized?"

To keep your boat sailing on a straight course you must keep adjusting your tiller and sails to conform to the changing conditions of wind and water. The wind is never constant. It not only changes in direction but also in velocity. Waves, although they normally flow in a general pattern, can approach your boat from several directions at once, making for a confused sea.

Move your tiller slowly to see what direction it causes your boat to take. To head the boat toward the wind, or luff, push the tiller away from you (remember, you're sitting on the windward side of the boat) towards the leeward side of the boat. Trim your sails in at the same time. Trimming the sails alone will help the boat head closer to the wind.

If you would like to steer away from the wind, pull the tiller towards you, to the windward side of the boat, and ease your sails.

While trimming your sails, watch the luff (the forward edge of the mainsail) just aft of the mast. Correct trim is when the wind flows evenly on both sides of the leading edge of the sail, with no luffing (flutter like a flag). (See figure 13.)

If the sail is luffing, trim in until it stops. When the sail is luffing you are moving slowly or slower than you should be. You'll gain speed by keeping your sails trimmed correctly at all times. This may mean easing the sail out slowly until you see the first sign of a luff near the mast. As a rule of thumb, a boat will sail faster as the sails are eased just short of letting them luff. Practice watching the luff of the sail to tell you what the wind is doing.

Puffs of wind will cross the water as you sail. The wind is constantly changing. A "puff" is an increase in the velocity of the wind. The first part of a puff is usually the strongest. When a puff hits your boat it will begin to heel over a little bit more. You can counteract the heeling force by leaning further over the side, easing your sails, or heading the boat closer to the wind.

Your goal is to use a combination of sail trim, steering, and your weight to counteract the forces of the wind. The first thing to do is to move your weight to the windward side of the boat and begin hiking out. If the boat still heels excessively, ease your sail. As a last resort, luff the boat into the wind by pushing the tiller to leeward.

Getting Out of Irons

Many beginning sailors end up "in irons." It happens to everyone at one time or another. The term in irons means a boat is stopped, pointing directly into the wind, having lost all headway. The boat will not sail off on either tack. Not to worry. Being caught in irons is an everyday occurrence. Just be patient. Relax.

The term irons came about during the great days of sail, when a battleship stuck in irons could not maneuver away from its foe and therefore was unable to escape the enemy in battle. The term refers to handcuffs, or leg irons, since the boat cannot move. A boat in irons was certain to be sunk as the enemy circled it. Captains were very careful to keep their boat from getting stuck in irons. Of course this was difficult since one error in sail trim could be fatal to the vessel. These great ships were slow to maneuver, taking as long as thirty minutes to tack. A boat in irons might be stuck for several hours.

Take your time getting out of irons. No one is going to attack your sailboat with cannon. To get out of irons, either wait until the boat is moving astern, or use the sails to push the boat away from the wind to get it moving again. Backing your sails can be helpful. To back a sail, push it to the other side of the boat, or try to fill the sail in one direction (see figure 14). Backing your jib in one direction or the other will force your bow away from the wind, putting the boat on a new course, one that will get the boat moving. Remember, when your boat is moving astern you steer in the opposite direction to when the boat is moving ahead. A well-balanced boat will more or less sail itself. A helmsman controls the boat and guides it along its course once the sails are set. Many sailors, particularly novices, over-correct for changes in the wind and deviations from the course steered.

Light boats are easy to maneuver because the

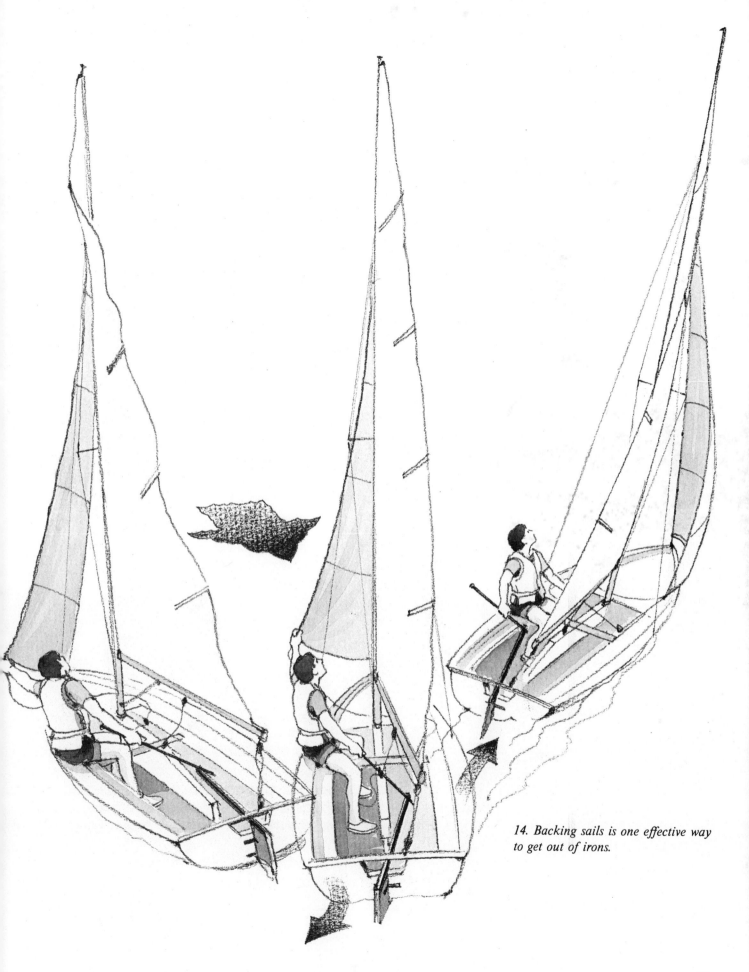

14. Backing sails is one effective way to get out of irons.

rudder is large compared to the weight of the boat. Therefore, you can rely on the rudder for all course changes. As a new sailor, you will find yourself using the rudder as a crutch. The key is to use the rudder in combination with your weight and the sails to help control and steer your boat.

Sailing with the Wind

Sailing with the wind, or running free, is one of the highlights of sailing. The boat stands upright and moves freely along, as the wind pushes the boat from astern. Running with the wind is particularly gratifying after a long haul to windward with the boat pounding into the waves, hiking for long periods of time, and tacking back and forth. Now you can sail freely. Like a cross-country skier coming to a slope, you simply stop trudging and let gravity take you along.

Sailing downwind is the goal of many sailors. Early skippers always made a point of sailing in the trade winds or winds that had a prevailing direction. They could be assured of sailing with the wind for long periods of time. This was particularly important in older sailing vessels since they could not sail very close to the wind going to windward.

When sailing downwind you will find a special feeling with the waves. As each one passes under your hull you will actually be able to gain speed.

Sailing with the wind can be the slowest point

of sailing in lighter airs. Pick the course that you would like to sail first by looking for an object to steer for in the water or on shore or simply by noticing which direction the wind is coming from. Then bear away from the wind by pulling the tiller toward the middle of the boat so that the wind swings the stern. Try to keep the wind flowing over a quarter of your boat so that you will remain in a stable condition (see figure 15). Moving the weight of your crew aft helps to get the bow to lift up out of the waves. Sailing downwind the boat will have a tendency to plow into the waves ahead of you. By moving your weight aft you'll avoid this.

Try to avoid sailing by the lee downwind. Sailing by the lee increases the likelihood of capsizing since the boat is potentially unstable. Sailing by the lee is when the wind is on the leeward side while the sails are still on the windward side.

A masthead fly or telltale can be particularly helpful when sailing downwind. Watching the direction from which the wind is coming helps you to steer. Masthead flys always tell the truth. Keep the wind over your quarter. If you feel the boat becoming unstable, starting to rock back and forth, head the boat toward the wind by pushing the tiller to leeward. This will help the boat to gain stability and control it. If the boat begins to rock back and forth try to keep your weight steady so that it does not accelerate the movement. Ease the sail out until the boom is at a right angle to the wind. The masthead fly should create a right angle with the position of the boom or the foot of the jib.

Sailboats can be difficult to steer dead downwind, particularly in lightweight dinghies, where the weight of the crew exceeds the weight of the boat. By reaching up slightly toward the wind the boat will gain stability and be easier to

15. *Greater stability is ensured by keeping the wind over the quarter when running.*

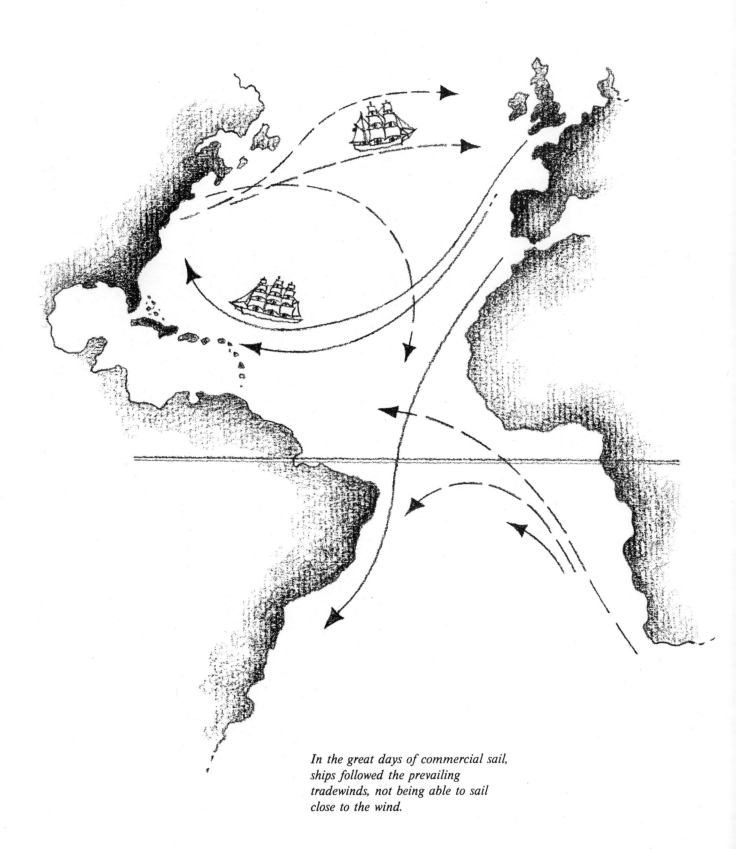

*In the great days of commercial sail,
ships followed the prevailing
tradewinds, not being able to sail
close to the wind.*

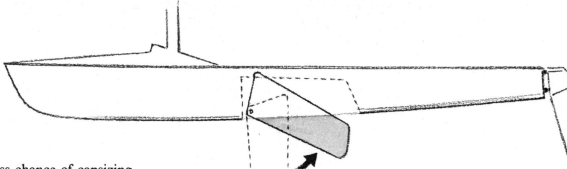

sail with less chance of capsizing.

Sailing with the wind will allow you to lift the centerboard. Centerboards are used to create lateral resistance when sailing to windward. To reduce the drag of the centerboard sailing downwind, simply raise it up out of the water. If the boat becomes unstable, lower the centerboard about a third of the way (see figure 16).

It can be dangerous to keep the centerboard all the way down in heavier air. The boat will begin to be steered by the centerboard instead of the rudder and you may lose control.

Position your crew until you do not feel any pressure on the helm—that is, your boat will maintain a steady course when you let go of the tiller. Your boat will heel slightly to windward (or to leeward) to balance the helm. Don't worry. This is normal. By balancing the helm the center of effort of the force of the wind on the sails becomes directly in a line over the center of resistance of the centerboard or keel (see figure 17).

Ease your sails out as far as you can without letting them luff. Keep easing the sail out 'til it just begins to luff, then trim it back in slightly to take the luffing action out of the sail.

In cat rigged boats (boats with one sail) sailing downwind is simply a matter of bearing away from the wind and easing the mainsail out. However, in a sloop (a boat with two sails) it will help to wing your jib to windward (see figure 18). This helps both sails to capture the air more efficiently. If the jib is kept to leeward—the side the mainsail is on—the main will block the wind from the jib. One crew member may hold the jibsheet on the windward side of the boat to

16. Partially lowering the centerboard increases stability when running.

17. Balance is achieved when the center of effort and the center of lateral resistance are in line.

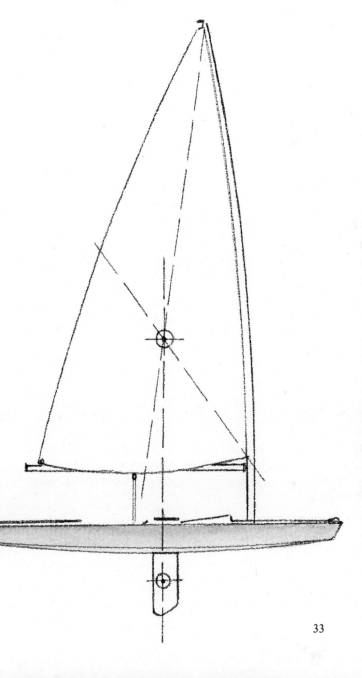

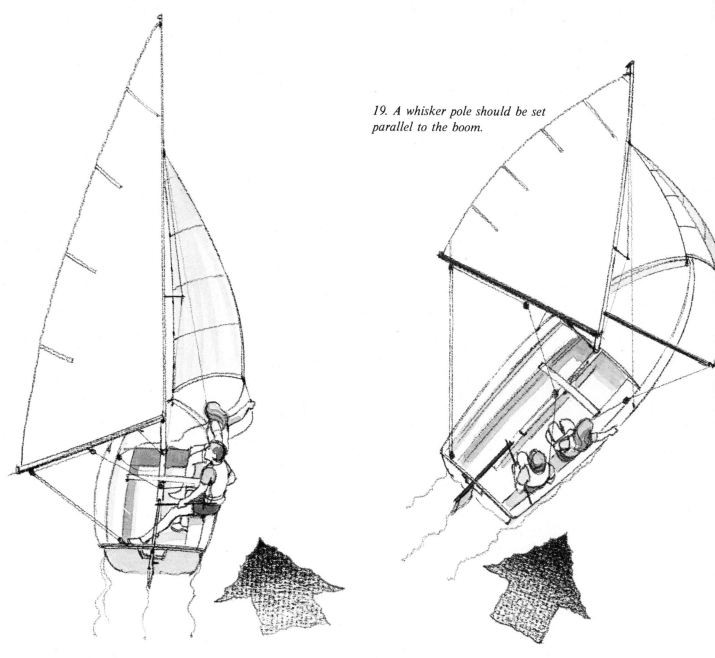

19. A whisker pole should be set parallel to the boom.

18. The crew can sit to windward to hold the jibsheet when running wing-and-wing.

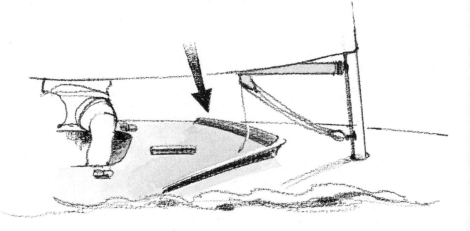

20. A splash rail will help keep the cockpit much drier.

capture the wind (see figure 18). A whisker pole is often used to extend the jib on the windward side. A whisker pole is attached to the mast and the clew of the sail with the sheet on the windward side trimmed in. Trim the whisker pole to keep it perpendicular to the wind, much like the boom. The whisker pole should be in line with the boom (see figure 19).

If the boat is pushing continually into the wave ahead, head up slightly so that you are sailing at an angle to the waves.

Some sailboats feel sluggish sailing downwind. The waves pass underneath the hull without the boat gaining any additional speed and the bow may plow into each wave passing under. A spinnaker can be particularly helpful in alleviating this problem. This is a balloon-shaped sail, similar to a parachute, and sometimes nicknamed "the chute." The spinnaker, because of its large size and efficient shape, is very effective in capturing the wind. Up to a 50 percent gain in speed is possible under a spinnaker. Also, the spinnaker helps lift the bow out of the water, keeping the boat from wallowing.

Most sailboats have a tendency to nosedive sailing downwind. This is especially evident with catamarans, but is true of all boats to some degree. The spinnaker can be helpful, although moving weight aft or steering a higher course, more on a reach, will also help.

A sailboat can surf, gaining extra speed as a wave passes under the hull. Although surfing requires considerable skill and practice, it will begin to happen whenever you encounter waves, or even after a powerboat passes by. You can get a sailboat surfing by steering it on a course perpendicular to a wave, then giving the boat acceleration by trimming the sail rapidly or shifting your weight forward. The first time you get a boat surfing on a wave is quite a thrill.

Sailing on a Reach

Sailing on a reach, the wind is from abeam, or hitting the boat from the side. Reaching is the fastest point of sailing.

A boat is on a "close reach" when the wind is forward of abeam. It is on a "beam reach" when the wind is directly abeam or hitting the boat at a 90 degree angle. A "broad reach" is when the wind is approaching the boat from aft abeam.

Sometimes it's difficult to steer a straight course when reaching, because the waves are probably approaching from abeam as well. In small, smooth seas no problem exists. However, in large, choppy seas difficulties can arise. You may need to adjust your course, either sailing higher or lower, to keep from rolling too much. Reaching, the boat will heel. Correct for this by sitting to windward, or lean out by putting your feet under the hiking straps until the boat is level. If the boat continues to heel too much, or you become tired from hiking all the time, ease the sail until it luffs a little. Or for temporary relief, head the boat into the wind to luff the sails. Or, steer a new course further away from the wind (more on a broad reach).

The centerboard should be about halfway down on a reach. If the centerboard is raised too much you will have a tendency to make leeway (the boat will move sideways). Too much centerboard will cause the boat to heel excessively, particularly in heavy winds. Reaching is the easiest point of sail to master. You have a good range of course to steer comfortably.

Sails should be eased as much as possible until they begin to luff. Then trim in just a little bit to keep them from luffing.

Sailing to Windward

Sailing to windward is exciting. The wind is in your face; the boat works through the waves like a car driving over a series of hills. Sailing to windward can also be good exercise: the crew must often hike over the windward side of the boat to help it stay on an even keel. Good leg and stomach muscles result.

Sailboats come alive when sailing or tacking to windward. The word tacking is used in several ways. The verb "to tack" means to alter course from one tack to the other, passing through the wind. Tacking is when a boat is sailing to windward, or beating. Since a sail luffs like a flag when heading directly into the wind, it is obvious that a boat cannot sail directly into the wind. Therefore, a sailboat must sail a course to windward by tacking back and forth to get from a downwind point to an upwind point (see figure 21).

21. Tacking to windward. With sails sheeted-in you can sail at an angle, into the wind.

Most modern sailboats will sail as close as 45 degrees to the wind, although America's Cup 12-Meter boats can sail as close as 30 degrees. Older sailing vessels could not sail closer than 60 degrees to the wind. The word "tack" is also used to describe the forward, lower corner of the sail or the action of attaching part of a sail to the boat or the boom. The words tacking or tack can be confusing. Use with care.

Sailing to windward takes concentration and skill to master but delivers great satisfaction. Many experienced helmsmen say they can *feel* a boat at its best while sailing to windward. By following several simple rules you will be able to sail a closehauled course close to the wind at optimum speed.

As a rule, the closer you sail to the wind the slower the boat will go. To head up into the wind, push the tiller towards the leeward side of the boat and trim your sail in so the end of the sail (the clew) is directly over the quarter of the boat (see figure 22).

Your goal is to sail as close to the wind as you can without allowing your sails to luff. To start off, watch the luff or leading edge of your mainsail along the mast and the luff of your jib, if you have one. Steer the boat so that your sails remain full, but keep testing your course by slowly heading the boat toward the wind. If the sails begin to luff, bear away from the wind until they fill again. This technique of steering is called

22. Trim your sail so that the clew is directly over the quarter.

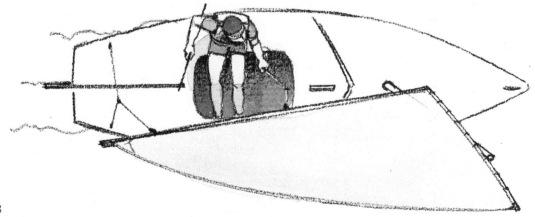

"scalloping," when the boat is constantly steered to change course so as to keep the boat sailing as close to the wind as possible.

Your sails are trimmed when the wind flows evenly on both sides of the sail. If the sail begins to luff, either trim in until it stops or, if the sail is already trimmed in all the way, bear away from the wind by pulling the tiller to the windward side of the boat until the sail fills.

Smaller sailboats, particularly centerboarders, sail best upright, with not more than five to ten degrees heel. Larger boats have a lead keel to help maintain a constant angle of heel. However, they are designed to heel to gain extra waterline length (see figure 23). Generally a longer waterline will help the boat go faster by creating a longer wave length. If the boat heels too far over it will begin to move sideways, or make leeway (sideslip). By using your weight and your crew's, or that of the keel, the boat can be kept sailing on its lines, at the optimum angle of heel. For keel boats twenty or twenty-five degrees is about right.

If the boat heels too much because of a sudden gust, or too much wind, reduce the angle of heel: remove some of your sails, flatten your sails to reduce their power, head into the wind, hike out further, or ease your sails. In puffy winds, ease your sails in a hard puff when the boat begins to heel too much. You'll discover that easing the sails and using your weight in combination with your steering will get you

23. Boat speed in a keelboat is directly proportional to the waterline length. As the boat heels, LWL, and thus speed, increases.

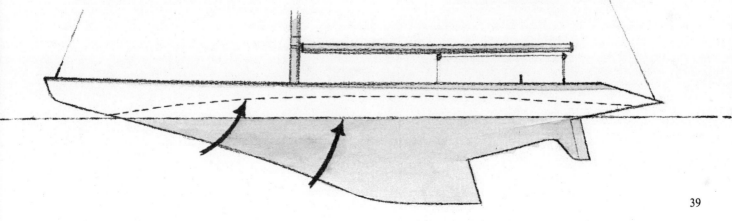

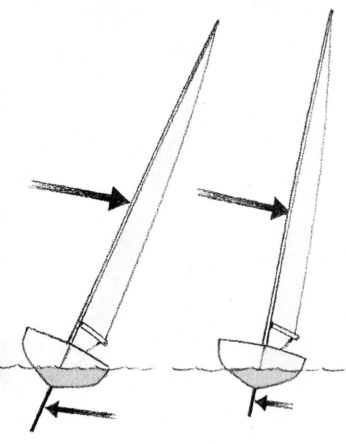

24. *Reducing centerboard area reduces heel.*

through the heaviest puffs while maintaining the same angle of heel. The gustier the wind, the more suddenly the boat will heel over. Windward helm is created by heeling. Windward helm is the tendency of a boat to round up into the wind when you let go of the tiller. The more the boat heels, or the greater the force on the sails, the more it will want to round up into the wind. Leeward helm occurs when you let go of the tiller and the boat steers away from the wind. This is particularly evident when a sailboat is heeling to windward. To reduce the windward helm force you have several options, including hiking out until the boat is flat, heading the boat slightly into the wind to flatten it, easing your sails, or flattening your sails. In addition, raking your mast forward, which may be beyond the scope of our lesson at this point, will help reduce windward helm. If your sailboat has leeward helm allow it to heel to leeward somewhat to return some windward helm in the boat. Most sailors prefer a slight amount of windward helm when sailing to windward. It gives you a natural tendency to scallop the boat into the wind.

The centerboard or keel is critical to a boat's performance to windward. If there were no centerboard or keel the force of the wind would

25. *A masthead fly will help you sail better to windward.*

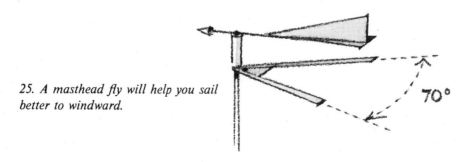

push the boat sideways. But the counteracting forces of the wind on the sail and the opposing force on the keel or centerboard force the boat to go forward. This is known as the lateral resistance of the centerboard. Raising the centerboard a few inches will help reduce your helm and your angle of heel. With a force of wind hitting your sail, the larger the centerboard the greater the heeling force. Reducing the area of your centerboard reduces the amount of heel (see figure 24).

Your telltales, or masthead fly, will help you sail to windward. The masthead fly will have two additional indicators extending from the center (see figure 25). The fly should flow in a direct line with these indicators. Spread the indicators apart at a 70 degree angle. This will tell you your apparent wind. There is a difference between the apparent wind and true wind. True wind is the actual direction the wind is blowing, whatever that may be. Apparent wind is the wind you feel while sailing on your boat. Because a sailboat is moving forward it creates its own wind. The wind you feel will be forward of the true wind. For example, if you were on a bicycle and were stopped with the wind approaching you from the side, you would feel the wind on your side. But once you start pedaling, the faster you go the more forward the wind will feel until it is directly ahead. The difference between the true wind and the wind your boat is creating is the apparent wind. The apparent wind will be at a 30 to 35 degree angle. The windier it is and the faster your boat is going the further forward the apparent wind will be. The direction of the apparent wind is difficult to judge, but the masthead fly will show it.

Your object when sailing to windward is to keep the boat moving at optimum speed, at the closest course to the wind, to get to your windward destination with all despatch.

26. *True wind is the actual direction the wind is blowing. Apparent wind is what you experience in a moving boat.*

Trimming Your Sails

Sails need constant trimming to keep them drawing air smoothly. The techniques are logical and simple if you follow a few basic principles.

Many adjustments can be made to the sails to give them any shape you may desire for each point of sailing in all wind strengths. With experience, you will be able to trim your sails effectively. Adjustments depend on what shape you are trying to achieve. First, it is important that whenever you are trimming sails, never cleat the line, especially in smaller boats. If a sudden gust of wind hits with the sheets cleated, you may not be able to ease the sails quickly enough to avoid capsizing. You can ease them at any time if you hold them.

To check if your sail is trimmed correctly, you first look at the luff (the part nearest the forward edge of the mast), which should be full at all times. Continually test the trim of the sail by easing it several inches. With the sail trimmed too tightly your boat will develop windward helm or the tendency to round up into the wind. In this case the boat is in a state of imbalance. Keep the boat balanced through your angle of heel and your sail trim. The best way to learn to sail to windward is with another boat alongside. You will feel more comfortable with another boat nearby. It also helps to give you a reference point—a benchmark. Many new sailors have difficulty getting the boat on a windward, close-hauled course the first time. Head the boat on a

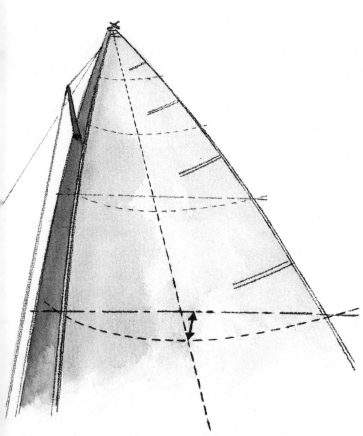

27. Look for draft and position of draft when trimming sails.

close-hauled course, using the second boat as a reference. Your sails may be be luffing at first, but trim them in until they stop. Counteract the heeling action by hiking out more and more as the sails are trimmed in. If you feel uncomfortable or the boat seems unstable, ease out your sail and try to maintain your close-hauled course. A normal reaction is to bear away from the wind without letting out. This will cause too much heel and windward helm.

Among the sail adjustments are the halyards. Halyards are either locked-off or cleated. Always haul the mainsail to the top of the mast at its maximum point. Jib halyards allow adjustment for sail shape. Generally, haul the halyard until the wrinkles are out of the sail. The downhaul is attached to the tack, the forward lower corner of the sail. Trim the downhaul until the wrinkles are just taken out of the sail. The next adjustment is the outhaul. The outhaul is attached to the clew of the sail at the lower after part of the sail— along the boom where the mainsheet is attached or where the jibsheet is attached. The outhaul has a tremendous effect on the shape of your sail. The mainsheet also has considerable control over the shape and trim of the sail.

Look for two things when trimming sails: how much draft or shape is in the sail, and also in what position that draft is (see figure 27). Normally, the maximum amount of draft (amount of curvature) in a sail should be directly in the middle of the sail with as much shape as you can put in and still keep the boat on an even keel (flat).

The more draft in a sail the less sail area will be exposed. In light winds the sail needs more draft to develop power. As the wind freshens, reduce the amount of draft in the sail so the boat stays under control. The determining factor is how hard it is to keep the boat flat. Baggy sails make it difficult to keep a boat on an even keel. On the other hand, a sailboat slows down when the sails are trimmed too tightly.

The best adjustment for positioning the draft is the mainsheet. If you ease the mainsheet the draft will go forward; if you trim the mainsheet the draft will move aft. By using your mainsheet you can trim the sails so the maximum amount of the draft is 50 percent of the way aft of the luff (see figure 27). Trimming sails is a skill and technique that can be a fascinating game which all sailors can play.

Steering with a Hiking Stick

The hiking stick, or tiller extension, allows the helmsman to sit closer toward the side of the boat, giving him greater visibility. Without it, the helmsman would have to sit in the middle of the boat. He could not see waves, wind, or sails working, particularly when the boat was heeled over.

A hiking stick can be held three ways: palm down on the hiking stick, palm up, lifting it into the air, or held across the body. Any of these techniques will work if the hiking stick is kept at a 90 degree angle to the tiller, and in the same plane as the tiller. Always keep the hiking stick parallel to your legs and arms. You'll be better organized. (See figure 28.)

Keep a firm grip on the hiking stick. You

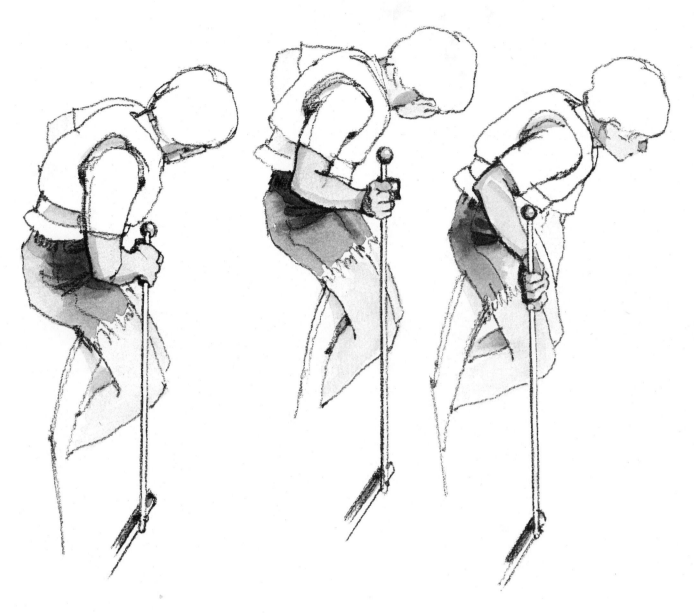

28. Three ways to hold a hiking stick.

control the boat. Try not to let the boat control you. Your actions to the rudder should be direct. If you hold the hiking stick too high in the air you will tend to over-steer. You want the boat to respond to your every action.

Watch your boat's wake to check your course. The bubbles coming off your rudder will form a line from its action through the water. This line of bubbles reflects your course. If you change course, you will be able to see it. By checking your wake occasionally you can see what kind of course you have steered.

Acceleration

Getting a sailboat moving at full speed takes coordination of sail trim, weight placement, balance, and steering. To start off, head the boat away from the wind on a close reach and trim your sails until they fill. Heel the boat to leeward, allowing the sails to take their shape. Simultaneously, pull the tiller toward you to counteract the action of trimming the sails. Trimming the main forces the boat to head up toward the wind. To counteract the force of the sails, pull the tiller to the windward side. This pulls the boat away from the wind. The resulting forces together push the boat forward.

To decelerate, or slow down, is easy. Many racing sailors have concentrated so much on going fast for years, they have never studied how to slow down. Yet it is important to be able to slow down when coming into a mooring, a dock, or approaching another boat. The technique of slowing down can be critical.

You slow a boat down by maneuvering. The faster you turn the boat the faster it will stop. Therefore, when you want to come into a dock or mooring, and you need to slow down, turn the boat sharply using the rudder (moving it all the way from one side to the other). The turn will absorb the speed of the boat. Heeling the boat excessively to leeward or windward will also slow the boat down. If you do not need to change course, simply ease the sails. Changing course

works best, however, since you are actually sailing a greater distance.

Always hold the mainsheet in your hand. Never put *any* sheet in your teeth. When a sheet is between your teeth you can't see where you are going and you can easily wrench a few loose. Besides, you may have to yell! Any time you trim a line, simply grab it at its source—generally at a block or fairlead—and make as long a trim as possible. Several long trims on a sheet are faster and more efficient than many short trims.

The harder you push the tiller over the faster the boat stops. This is because the rudder actually slows the boat down as it turns sideways to your course, but because the rudder is in the water and at the aft end it also helps steer the boat. Changing course will slow you down, even if the wind stays in the sails. On the other hand, if you need to maintain speed, change course slowly.

To head away from the wind, or bear off, pull the tiller to windward and ease your sails out. Keeping the sail over-trimmed may cause the boat to round up back into the wind, and you will have difficulty bearing off on a new course. When sails are over-trimmed, and you are bearing off, the boat will have a tendency to heel too much to leeward, possibly capsizing. Ease your sails as quickly as you can whenever you are bearing off.

Heading up toward the wind, use the sails to help you. Trim in the sail as you round up. This forces the boat into the wind. You can use your sails effectively to steer your boat. Sailors have been able to cross the ocean without a rudder, using the sails alone to steer.

A good exercise for the beginning sailor is the "serpentine" or "follow the leader" drill. One boat acts as the leader and each boat in the fleet must sail directly astern of the leader. If the leader accelerates, the rest of the fleet must accelerate. If the leader slows down, the rest of the fleet slows down. By working together in a group you will feel more confident and relaxed. Like a football team working out as a squad, running wind sprints by yourself is no fun.

If you are sailing by yourself, practice maneuvering around a set of anchored buoys. Any time you are planning a maneuver, run through the actions in your mind first. Think each function through by the numbers. What part of the boat do you sit in? Where do you go? What do you hold on to? How much should you trim? When do you ease? How much and how fast should you push the tiller over? Where should you move your weight? Concentrate on maneuvering in wide open waters and you will be ready to maneuver quickly and confidently in more restricted spaces. The secret to maneuvering is having as much speed through the water as possible prior to changing your course. Be patient and get the boat moving at full speed before starting a maneuver.

Tacking

Tacking a boat is changing course from one tack, either port of starboard, to the other. The word *tacking* is the same for being on a tack and can be confusing. *Starboard tack* is when the wind is coming over the starboard, or the right-hand, side of the boat. The boom is always on the port side of the boat when on a starboard tack. This applies, and is particularly important, when the wind is dead behind the boat and you are running. A boat is on port tack when the wind is coming over the port, or left-hand, side of the boat.

Sail the boat on a close-hauled course with the sails trimmed in all the way. To change course to head on the opposite tack, first inform the crew that you will be tacking. The command is "Ready about." Before tacking, sight across the boat on the windward side to see the new course. Line up your new course with an object on shore or an object on the water as a reference point. Before tacking be sure your new course is clear of other boats. The Rules of the Road specifically state that a boat tacking must stay clear of other boats. Rules will be discussed later.

Remember, whenever you maneuver you must maintain speed in order to maintain steerage. Therefore, maneuvers should be carried out quickly. To tack, push the tiller to leeward slowly until the boat begins to head into the wind. As the boat heads into the wind (luffs), push the tiller over faster. At the same time trim in the mainsheets. This will make for a cleaner tack. To illustrate this try luffing your sails, and let your tiller go. Leaving your hands off the tiller, trim in your sails. You'll find the boat rounds up into the wind.

Changing sides of the boat can be particularly tricky if you are handling both mainsheet and tiller. Crossing from one side of the boat to the other when tacking, take as few steps as possible. In dinghies only one step is necessary. Changing hands can be hard as well. You must hold on to the tiller and mainsheet while you are going to tack, and you must also change sides and hands. Keep your sheets uncleated so they do not get

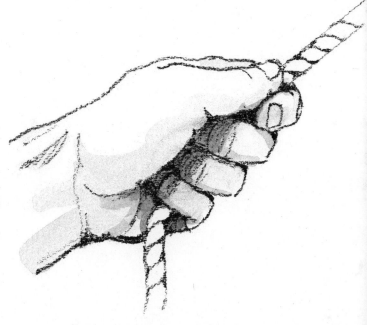

29. Keep the mainsheet firmly in hand for best control.

caught on the tack. Hold on to the tiller as long as possible, keeping the boat under control. If you let go of the tiller too soon, the boat has a good chance of spinning out and possibly capsizing. As you change sides, bring the hand holding the mainsheet back to the tiller, keeping the mainsheet in that hand. For a split second one hand will hold both the mainsheet and the tiller. At this point exchange hands. The mainsheet and the tiller will be under control at all times (see figure 30).

Face forward during your tack. You will see where you are going and be able to shift your weight to keep your boat on an even keel. Common errors in tacking are holding the tiller over to one side too long and not changing hands soon enough.

As you complete your tack, sail the boat on the mainsail while the crew trims the jib. The action of the wind on your sails (whether you are luffing or not) tells you if you are on your new course. You must concentrate on where you are heading and what is happening to your sails. As soon as the boat is on its new course put the tiller back to the middle of the boat. Many sailors make poor tacks because they hold the tiller over too long. On the other hand, many sailors return the tiller to amidships too soon and the boat ends up being stuck head to wind, running the risk of ending up in irons. How fast you push the tiller over to the other side depends on the boat you are sailing, the wind strength and how fast you need to turn the boat. The stronger the wind the faster you must turn to reduce the time it slows the boat. In many cases the boat will start heeling too much, causing it to go sideways. This movement is called "making leeway." Heavier boats are turned slowly because they keep their momentum

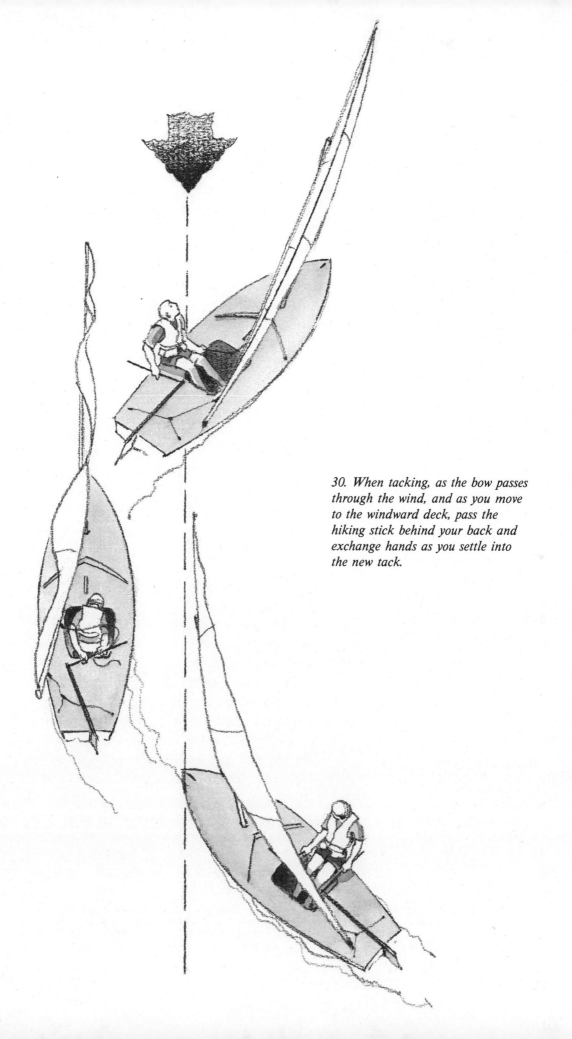

30. When tacking, as the bow passes through the wind, and as you move to the windward deck, pass the hiking stick behind your back and exchange hands as you settle into the new tack.

up while lighter boats lose their momentum as soon as they begin to turn. Therefore, they must turn more quickly.

Jibing

Jibing is the changing of tacks while running. Jibing is one of sailing's greatest challenges. A greater possibility of capsizing exists while jibing than at any other time. Since the sail shifts sides so rapidly, it is important to duck at the right moment to avoid being hit in the head by the boom. It takes many beginning sailors a couple of good bumps before learning this important lesson.

The boat will feel unstable when sailing downwind, particularly if it is a centerboarder. Jibe quickly so as not to stay in this unstable condition for long. To jibe, bear off so the boat is sailing straight downwind. At this point keep your sail over-trimmed slightly—otherwise the force may cause you to tip over. Heeling to windward the boat can capsize to windward on top of you. Heeling to leeward and over-trimmed, the boat will round itself up into the wind. In light breezes you may change course quickly and pull the boom across the boat on to the new tack. However, as the breeze stiffens, the boom will fly across violently. An accidental jibe can wipe out your rig.

In one regatta in San Francisco we were sailing cat rigged boats. All twelve competitors

capsized at a jibe mark. The real race became
how fast you could right your boat. I remember
that the twelfth person to tip over came screaming
in on a reach in a 35 knot gust going into a jibe,
with the rest of us all trying to right our boats
and watching the fellow. He started to jibe but
lost control at the last second as his bow buried
into a wave and the boat pitch-poled, throwing
the skipper head over heels into the water—to the
applause of all the rest of us who had reached a
similar fate just moments before.

There is also the story of the Hudson River
sloop captain who discovered an interesting jibing
technique for boats with large mains. This captain
was sailing his loaded vessel down the Hudson
River when it came time to jibe for navigational
reasons. The helmsman pushed the tiller over too
far and the boat went on a flying jibe. Considering
the boom on this boat was over sixty feet long
with a forty-foot gaff, it looked as if the sail was
going to continue out on the new side and take
the mast with it. But the gods being with this
sailor allowed for the sail to simply back itself as
it fluttered into place. Did this captain discover
the jibe by accident or plan it? I think he found
out by accident. It might be a good technique for
you to use any time you are sailing in a boat with
over five thousand feet of area in the mainsail.

Try to keep the boat flat when jibing. Put the
centerboard down halfway. Too little board will
allow the bottom to spin out from under the mast,
too much board will cause the board to steer the
boat and tip it. Keep your weight aft during the
jibe in heavier air so your bow does not dip into
the water. Important: change hands early in a jibe
so you do not get twisted up in the boat. If you
are forward of the tiller, it can be moved by
passing it from one hand to the other behind you.

After the jibe, resume your normal course as

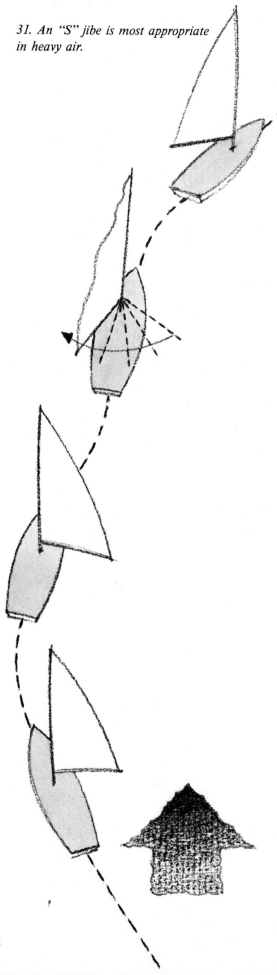

31. An "S" jibe is most appropriate in heavy air.

soon as possible. Staying dead downwind helps keep the boat off balance. If the boat seems to be out of balance head up, heeling the boat slightly to leeward until you are under control. Hold on to the tiller while jibing to keep the boat from spinning out. Getting your boat moving quickly is difficult. The heavier the boat, the longer it will take to accelerate. A square-rigger will take minutes before it is moving at full speed. Even a 12-Meter sloop will sometimes take a full minute to get up to top speed. A smaller boat, like a Sunfish, can easily reach top speed in ten seconds. To accelerate a boat keep it on course as close to a reach as possible. Trimming your sails to the desired point and keeping the boat flat are essential. These combined forces will help the boat to sail at full speed.

There are two methods of jibing. One is the "S" jibe, used when the wind is blowing hard and there is a chance of capsizing. This technique involves getting the boom over to the opposite tack and the heading of the boat changed. You control the jibe by steering your boat through an "S" pattern while jibing. Once the sail is on its new side head up to your new course with the boat completely under control. (See figure 31.)

When there is little sea and it is calm, use the roll jibe. The advantage of this technique is that you can jibe the boat without changing course and accelerate rapidly. Basically, you sail dead downwind or slightly by the lee. Roll your boat to leeward about 10 degrees, then roll it hard to windward, giving a rapid trim on the mainsheet and have the crew throw the boom over. When the sail is just reaching the other side, roll the boat back to windward. You are, in effect, rocking the sail from one side to the other. This method will take considerable practice to master.

Meeting an Obstruction

If an obstruction or another boat is in your path you must maneuver to stay clear. Always keep a sharp lookout when you approach another boat—don't lose sight of it. Best pass astern as a rule, though on starboard tack you have the right-of-way and will be the privileged boat. A yacht on port tack is obligated to stay clear. Remember that many sailors do not know the rules and are uncertain what to do. Any time it looks close, stay clear and avoid a collision.

The Rules of the Road were written with the intention of keeping boats from collision. That is the spirit you should sail for. If you find that you need to change course, a large course change is better than a small one. The boat you are approaching will notice a larger course change. Hail the other boat and shout your intentions clearly. Better to pass to leeward. It minimizes your chances of collision.

Sometimes, you'll find obstructions to either side. Such a situation can be pretty scary, especially when rocks or some other solid object form the leeward hazard. In such a case, try to get the boat to windward to understand your predicament. If he can tack, then you can follow. If he won't give you the right-of-way, tack, and then let your sails luff; when the other boat is past, you can harden-up and continue on the new tack.

Capsizing

No one really wants to capsize, but if you sail long enough your time will come. If you do not capsize at least once a year when sailing a dinghy you are not being aggressive enough. There's nothing to fear once you know the causes of capsizing and how to handle the situation. As long as you wear a life jacket, you really have nothing to worry about. Learning to sail in cold water wear a wet suit. Hypothermia, which is the exposure of the body to cold for a long period of time, can be very dangerous. Even in the late spring or early fall, the water cools rapidly and survival becomes more difficult in cold water. People are confused when they capsize in the first place and cold water adds to the trauma.

Capsizing is usually caused by too much wind for the amount of sail being carried; by improper balance of the crew; by jibing in a strong wind with the centerboard up too far; by not keeping the boat under control at all times; by being caught in rapidly shifting winds (both in velocity and direction); and simply by not paying attention. If your boat begins to capsize to windward, lean into the boat to get it on an even keel again. Trimming your main in will also help to heel the boat to leeward. Heading the boat into the wind by pushing the tiller toward the sail will help in this case. To counteract a leeward capsize simply ease the sails out so they begin to luff while heading the boat up into the wind. Hiking

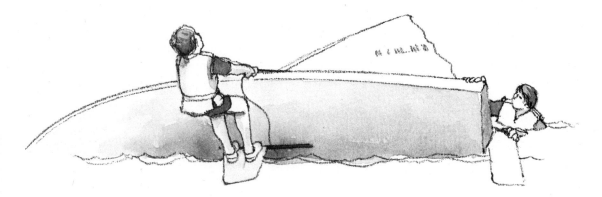

32. The centerboard can be used as a lever to help right a capsized boat.

out will also help to keep the boat flat, compensating for the angle of heel. Once the boat gets too far over, the action of the rudder will be ineffective. Therefore, it is important to prevent a capsize early.

If you do capsize there are several rules of thumb to follow. Of course your pride may be slightly injured, but safety is what counts. Once in the water, stay with the boat. Even if you are unable to right it, *never* leave the boat. This applies to all members of the crew. You should stay with your boat until you have righted it and are able to sail again, or another boat comes along to help.

To right the capsized boat, first put the boat head to wind. If the sail is pointing into the wind the boat is likely to capsize once again while it is being righted. Use the centerboard as a lever (see figure 32). Stand on the middle of the centerboard to help right the boat. Be sure your sheets are uncleated so as the boat pops up your sails will not fill causing the boat to go over once again. Keep your sheets free on all sails.

33. A combination of jib sheet and centerboard can right a boat that's turned turtle.

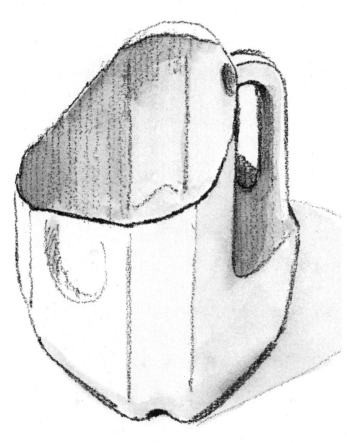

34. A boat bailer or cut-down plastic jug should be on board.

As your boat comes up, grab the side and continue to pull until the boat is completely upright. Try not to make a mad dash to get on board the boat, as you will probably want to; the sharks won't get you yet. Instead, hold on to the side of the boat and rest for a moment to regain your energy. The toughest thing will be climbing back into the boat. When you have rested and feel strong enough pull yourself into the middle of the boat. If the mast begins to sink and the boat turns turtle, putting a life jacket under the tip of the mast will help to keep it floating. However, if the boat does turtle, using one jib sheet (see figure 33) and pulling on the board will slowly bring the boat back. If the mast is wedged tightly in the mud the only solution may be the assistance of another boat. Have this boat anchor directly upwind and throw a line to you. Eventually, the force of the wind and the waves will pivot your boat into the wind, pulling the mast out of the mud, and making it easy to right. Training boats are often equipped with styrofoam sewn into the head of the sail to prevent the mast from turtling.

If the boat is swamped, sit down and begin to bail her out. Keep one person in the water to steady the boat. If the rail is awash with one person in, best keep everyone in the water. A tow boat can help get the water out. First, let your sails down and secure all equipment to prevent it from floating away. Have the rescuing boat throw you a line. Attach it to a foredeck cleat or around the base of the mast. The water will begin to empty out. Have your boat towed straight into the wind at a slow speed. Keep the centerboard up. You may capsize again if the centerboard is down. Water-filled boats are very unstable. Handle with care. Keep your life jacket on. If you weren't wearing one when you capsized, put one on now. You may find swimming more difficult, but at least you will be safe. A life jacket will also help keep you warm. Most life jackets sold are wearable devices and Coast Guard-approved.

The key to preventing a capsize is to pick a safe course to sail. Sailing straight downwind is most likely to cause capsizing. The boat is unstable to begin. A sudden gust of wind from a different direction may cause an accidental jibe. If you are not quick enough the boat will capsize and dump you. Stay alert at all times.

If trapped under the sail after a capsize, swim in a straight line until you reach the end of the sail. Look around for any equipment that may be starting to float away from you. In boats with daggerboards be sure to use a shock cord attached to the boat to keep the boards in the trunk. Head into the wind a little more if your boat feels unstable. When a swamped boat is being towed have at least one person hold onto the stern to keep the bow from nosediving and to balance the boat. As the boat is towed the bow will rise and the water will pour over the stern. Many boats built today are self-righting and easy to pop up following a capsize. If you are learning in this type try to capsize on your own to get the feeling of what it is like.

Keel boats do not capsize; they broach. Once a keel boat heels over too far the wind spills from the sails and the weight of the keel rights the boat again. Keel boats are most likely to broach sailing downwind with spinnakers. The heavier the keel, the more forgiving the boat.

Many capsizes are caused by too much boom vang. If the boom vang is eased when your sail is let out the wind will spill out of the top of the sail. Treat a capsize seriously.

Remember that a capsize turns you into an unmaneuverable object. You float there at the mercy of other boats, some of whom may not be able to see you. If you can't right your boat immediately, always stay with it.

The Wind

You cannot see the wind but you can read the signs. Observe what the wind does to flags on shore, trees, wind pennants, smoke from stacks, clouds, other boats, and the angle and intensity of the ripples on the water. You'll be able to predict what's about to happen.

Your face, neck, and ears are very sensitive to changes in wind direction and strength.

Wind Indicators

Telltales are good wind indicators. Make them from strips of yarn attached to the rigging and sails. The best places are the top of the mast, shrouds, and on the sails themselves (see figure 35). They should be about six inches long and as thin as possible to flow easily. Red is the best color as it contrasts against the sails. Polyester is better than wool since it's water resistant.

When putting telltales on your sails place them along the luff six inches from the forward edge. Space your telltales equally with one at the top, one in the middle, and one at the bottom.

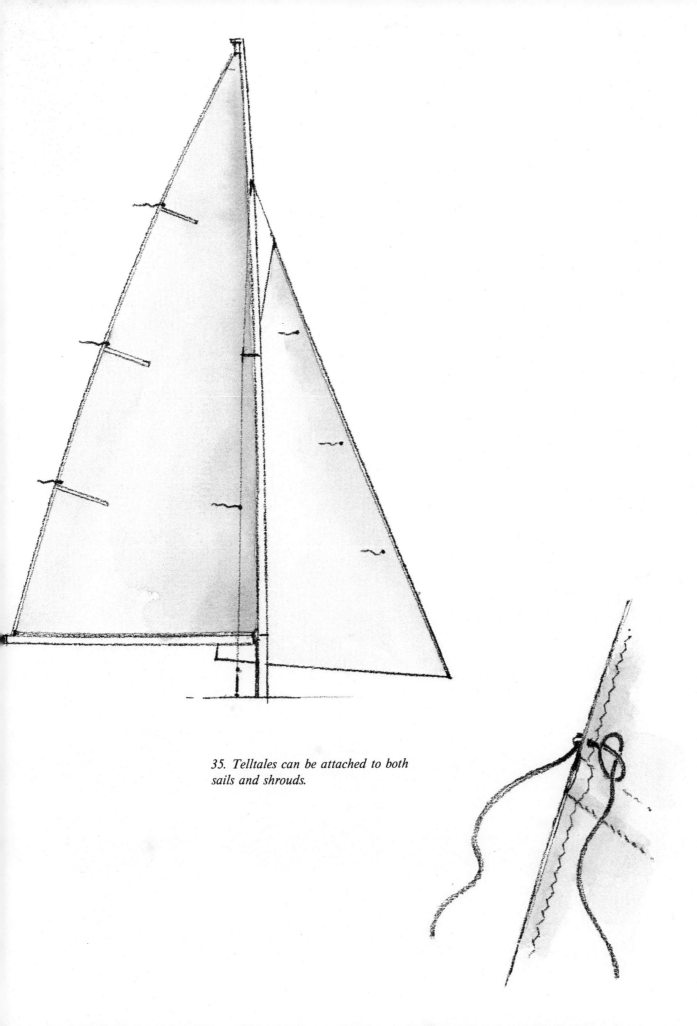

35. *Telltales can be attached to both sails and shrouds.*

Telltales are also helpful on the outer edges of the sail, particularly along the back.

To attach the telltale to your sail use a needle with yarn through it and poke a tiny hole in the sail. Even up the length of the telltale on either side and tie a knot so it will stay in place (see figure 36).

When the wind is flowing smoothly on both sides of the sail and the sails are trimmed correctly, the windward and leeward telltales will flow straight aft. If the boat is pointing too close to the wind or the sail is undertrimmed, the windward telltale will flutter up and down. Change your course away from the wind (bear away) or trim your sails in until both telltales flow aft.

If your boat is pointing too low or the sail is overtrimmed (trimmed too tightly), the leeward telltale will flutter up and down. Head closer to the wind or ease your sails out until both telltales luff evenly.

Telltales indicate what the wind is doing relative to your boat, or the direction and intensity of the apparent wind. Apparent wind is the actual wind caused by the movement of your boat through the water.

The wind changes higher up first and follows set patterns during the day. Watch your masthead fly to see what the wind will do. With practice, you will be able to forecast the wind. Try to predict what the wind will do as it approaches your boat. Determine how much velocity it will have and what the direction will be. You will get a feeling for the patterns of the wind. Studying the wind will become a habit. You will gain experience and be able to forecast the wind accurately.

Although people smile at old wives' tales, they

can be useful when forecasting the wind. Cornelius Shields of Long Island Sound put together a paper several years ago titled *Corny Shields' Lore of Long Island Sound.* Some of his old wives' tales are helpful. Dew in the morning means an early strong wind. Cobwebs in the rigging mean a northwester in the near future.

Pay attention to the water. By matching the different colors in the water with the constant color of the sail, your boat, or an object on land, you will be able to note the differences in the wind. This will help you read the direction of the puffs, when the wind will shift, and where the lulls in the wind are.

When watching the wind use both eyes and let your eyes relax. Blink often and try not to stare. Concentrate on one section of the horizon at a time rather than making sweeping glances.

Watch the Weather

Before I go sailing I call the National Weather Service to get their report. I find that they are generally accurate in most parts of the country. Radio stations, particularly in cities along the coast, have regular boating forecasts. Forecasters usually mention the barometric pressure, which indicates variation in air pressure. The direction and rate of change of the barometric pressure is important when forecasting weather. Foul weather is usually forecast by a falling barometer with

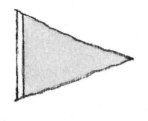

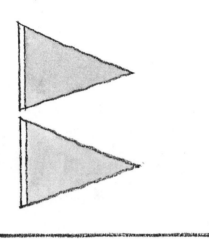

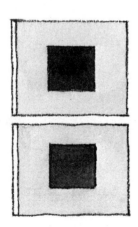

*37. Storm warnings (from top):
small craft advisory, gale warning,
storm warning, hurricane warning.*

winds from the east. Clearing and fair weather are forecast by a rising barometer with winds shifting to the west.

Weather changes are caused by the wind. A rapidly falling barometer forecasts the development of strong winds or a storm. A rising barometer is associated with lighter winds. A steadily falling barometer normally indicates unsettled or wet weather.

Clouds are also helpful indicators in checking the weather. In general, thickening and lowering cloud layers are a sign of approaching wet weather. When layers of clouds show holes and openings or are frayed and indistinct at the edges, this indicates improving weather or a delay in the development of foul weather. An old adage says: Red sky at night, sailors delight; red sky at morning, sailors take warning. There are many helpful indicators, including the following:

    a. bright blue sky: fair weather
    b. dark, gloomy sky: windy
    c. bright yellow sky at sunset: wind
    d. sunrise from a gray horizon: fair day
    e. weak and washed-out sun: rain in the future
    f. sunset with diffused and glaring white
       clouds: storm
    g. ring around the moon: rain
    h. soft clouds: fine weather with light to
       moderate wind
    i. hard-edged, oily clouds: wind
    j. small, inky clouds: rain

Be familiar with the coastal warning displays issued by the U.S. Weather Service. These indicate foul weather. The following displays are normally shown at marinas, yacht clubs, and Coast Guard stations:

Small craft advisory. One red pennant displayed by day and one red light above a white light at night. Indicates wind up to 33 knots and sea conditions dangerous to small craft.

Gale warning. Two red pennants displayed by day and a white light above a red light at night. Indicates winds ranging from 39 to 54 mph.

Storm warning. A single square red flag with black center displayed by day and two red lights at night. Indicates winds 55 mph and above.

Hurricane warning. Two square flags with black centers displayed by day and a white light between two red lights at night. Indicates winds 74 mph and above.

What do You Wear?

At a cocktail party, the typical sailor wears white duck pants, blue blazer, Topsiders (no socks, of course), rumpled shirt, and one of a variety of yacht club ties. At a lecture I recently gave, a woman came up to me and said she enjoyed the talk but had to admit the real reason she came to the lecture was to see my shoes. I did not disappoint her as I was wearing my normal beat-up and salty Topsiders (no socks, of course).

What counts is the clothing you wear on the water. In no other sport is there a greater variety of clothing, ranging from nothing at all (as I found sailing in St. Tropez) to wearing every stitch of clothes you own. On one race from Chicago to Mackinac Island I was shivering in my bunk waiting for the next watch at 3:30 A.M. One of the crew came below to wake our watch and informed us, "Put on everything you have." I was *already* wearing everything I had, and it was a cold morning.

One of the secrets to sailing well is to be comfortable while on the water. Although foul weather gear is an expensive investment, it's worth it.

Wear sneakers or non-skid shoes with soft soles at all times. Although I generally don't wear socks on shore, I always wear them while sailing to give me better traction. It is a bad habit to sail barefoot, since you may lose your balance.

There are many styles of boots. On offshore yachts, calf-high boots are best. For dinghy sailing, wear boots that fit tightly around the ankle. These are particularly comfortable for hiking.

In warm weather, wear light clothing but keep in mind that the sun, particularly on hazy days, can give you severe sunburn. The sun's rays are intensified as they reflect off your sails. Therefore, stay covered for a good portion of the day. It doesn't take long to get sunburned. Use a tanning lotion. Zinc oxide is the best sun-blocking agent. It is better to use too much sun tan lotion than too little. I have seen the rays burn through t-shirts.

If you become overheated, cool off by drinking water or simply by splashing cold water on the back of your neck.

Your eyes are particularly sensitive to the sun. I recommend always wearing sunglasses on the water during the day. Polarized sunglasses are the best. Even on cloudy days there is considerable glare on the water. Sunglasses help you see better by contrasting the color of the water. This will help you read the wind. The sun can burn your eyes just like your skin; this is dangerous and it may take weeks for your eyes to recover. After sailing all summer in 1977 my eyes turned red and stayed that way for six months. It taught me to wear sunglasses on the water. Let my lesson save you from the same fate.

Constant exposure to the sun and wind also ages your skin. Sun creams help counteract this.

Headgear (hat and visor) is helpful in sunny weather because it shades you from the sun and helps keep you cool. In cold weather, a hat is important since a great deal of body heat escapes from your head. I find the best hats in cold weather are woolen ski hats because they stay on your head with a tight elastic band and are designed for warmth.

An oiled woolen sweater is particularly good in cold weather since it resists water. I generally wear a t-shirt underneath my sweater to absorb perspiration. If you are hiking on a dinghy, long pants help to cushion your legs from the deck of the boat.

But be careful. If you end up in the water all of this clothing soaks up water and restricts your maneuverability. To counteract all of this weight it is best to wear a life jacket so that you will stay up in the water.

Float coats are popular because they keep you warm and provide flotation if you do go into the water. Some sailors use a float coat with a strobe light sewn into a pocket in case they fall overboard at night. Some sailors sew a safety harness into the coat as well. Short cut jackets can be annoying, as they ride up and leave part of your back exposed. Longer float coats are best since they stay down.

There are many excellent brands of foul weather gear on the market. Find a set that fits you comfortably, slightly loose so that it is easy to move around in, and yet able to keep you dry in all kinds of weather. There really is no substitute for a good set of foul weather gear. For dinghy sailing a one-piece suit is best. For larger boats a

38. Foul weather gear, proper footwear, sunglasses and a hat are necessities.

two-piece suit with chest-high pants is better. Criss-cross the straps of the pants in the front and back so they do not fall off your shoulders. This can be annoying when you are wearing a jacket over your pants. Pick a foul weather jacket with a good hood and a front designed to prevent rain from trickling in. Traditionally, foul weather gear is bright yellow, orange, or green so that a person can be easily spotted if he falls in the water. I favor sweaters or chambray shirts instead of heavy jackets underneath my foul weather gear, since they permit greater movement.

One of the greatest dangers in sailing is hypothermia. This is a lowering or raising of the body temperature caused by loss of heat at a rate faster than the body can produce it. The body starts shivering involuntarily to produce more heat. Hypothermia often occurs when the temperature is between 30° and 50° F., since that is when people least expect it and don't take precautions. I once spent a day on the water when the temperature never went above 35° F. and was so excited about being out on the boat that I didn't realize how cold I was until the day was over. Later I spent the entire night shivering.

Hypothermia often occurs hours before the first symptoms appear. In my case it was two hours before I started to shiver and I was sick for two days. When you are cold you lose coordination, don't think clearly, and become disoriented. This is not a good situation to have on board a sailboat. The key is to wear the right clothes and stay warm and dry. The chill factor goes down rapidly as the wind increases, and accelerates even faster when a person is wet.

The warmest clothes are thermal underwear and socks under wool pants and shirt, topped off with goose down vests or jackets. Wool is unique because it keeps you warm even when it gets wet.

Wind takes heat away from the body and even a light breeze can reduce the air temperature between the layers of clothing. Ideally, the outer layer of clothing should act as a windbreaker, keeping the wind and water away from the body.

The goal is to contain as much body heat as possible. Many sailors wear a towel around their neck to keep water from trickling in. Gloves can be useful, particularly on long passages. Try to plan your sail in advance so you can take the right clothes with you. In boats that are particularly wet, a wetsuit will keep you warm and comfortable, and also offers some flotation. A wetsuit prevents hypothermia and should be used on wet boats when the water temperature dips below 72° F. In a wetsuit, a thin layer of moisture develops between the rubber wetsuit and your body and becomes warm. Wear foul weather gear over your wetsuit in particularly cold weather.

You should wear foul weather clothing that permits easy movement in the boat. On a recent ocean race, Richie Boyd, crew member of *Tenacious* said, "The worst thing about sailing is all the different kinds of clothing you have to wear. It seems that every time I go on watch I have a different set of clothes to put on."

Finally, always take a change of clothing with you and a towel so you can shower after your sail. Remember, the pleasure of sailing is directly proportional to your comfort. Proper clothing for different weather conditions makes it that much more worthwhile.

39. A thermos of hot soup keeps out the chill and guards against hypothermia.

Seasickness

Seasickness is one of the hazards of sailing. It happens to many sailors, particularly at night. Some people are more prone to it than others, but no one ever escapes it entirely. A primary cause of seasickness is becoming overheated or chilled. It is important to wear the right clothing to maintain normal body temperature. Early symptoms of seasickness are nausea, overheating, or feeling uncomfortable just moving around. Swallowing helps, although chewing gum doesn't since it creates too much saliva. The first thing to do when you start feeling ill is to get some fresh air. Try to be active on the boat but relax. Don't be uptight about it. Fighting it off can make it worse. Often when you are feeling seasick you may not have eaten for a while; it may help to eat saltine crackers and drink a non-carbonated beverage. There are pills you can take, including Bonine and Dramamine, although sometimes they make you drowsy. If you do get seasick, head for the leeward rail. Acidic foods, carbonated beverages, and greasy foods all help to induce seasickness. Try to avoid them while sailing.

One of the best remedies for seasickness is Bucladin. This is a prescription drug that seems not to cause drowsiness, and lasts for approximately six hours. Its advantage over other remedies is that it can be taken *after* you're at sea. Check with your doctor.

You Are
What You Eat

How well you eat determines how well you sail. The night before you sail, try to avoid exotic foods. Alcohol and acidic (gas-producing) or greasy foods are harmful. Try to eat foods that store energy. Carbohydrates are best, such as pasta, potatoes, and bread. It is best to have a good, solid breakfast about two to three hours before you go out so that you will have plenty of stored energy for the day's sail. Eat lightly if you are tense. On the water it is best to drink water and iced tea in hot weather; hot soup is best when the weather is cold. Stay away from carbonated beverages, as they produce gas. Sugary foods are good for short bursts of energy but in the long run they are fatiguing.

Running Aground
and Refloating

If you run aground, which is easy to do in shallow waters, there are two steps to take. The first is to refloat by force; the second is to reduce the draft of your boat. Running aground can be embarrassing, particularly when the tide is ebbing (going out), because you may be left for many hours in shallow water. If you do run aground, try to refloat your boat as quickly as possible. Knowing your waters will help you to avoid shallow areas.

To reduce the draft of the boat it may help to have the crew jump overboard or bail the boat out. Shifting your weight and heeling it to one side or the other is also helpful. Or, move your weight all the way forward or all the way aft. When a boat heels to leeward it does not draw as much water. Try to keep the bow pointed toward the deeper water if possible. Careening the boat over on its side by attaching a halyard to an anchor may do the trick. In some cases, the only answer is waiting for higher tide. If your bow is pointed toward shallow water try to retrace your original course to escape the shoal. If you are in a boat with a centerboard, raise the board and try to free the boat.

To force a boat off a shoal, push the boat along the path you just sailed, using an oar or spinnaker pole. Using an anchor as a kedge also helps to turn the boat. Going overboard may have to be used as a final resort. If you are in a boat with an engine, turning it on may help. When sailing in waters with muddy or sandy bottoms running aground will not cause much damage. However, on a rocky shore check for leaks. If the boat is leaking, stuff a life jacket or cushion in the leak to minimize the water you take in.

40. Setting an anchor out to heel the boat when grounded is called kedging.

Mooring

A mooring is a buoy anchored in a spot where you may keep your boat. Many yacht clubs, marinas and city harbors have moorings where you may stay temporarily for a fee. Moorings help protect your boat since they are in sheltered waters. A moored boat is generally a safe one, since it swings round and can't hit other boats no matter what the wind direction is.

A mooring consists of an anchor, a chain, a mooring pendant and a buoy. Usually, each mooring has a distinctive mark (generally a number or color) so you can tell one from the other. Moorings are usually away from the main channel and rapid currents.

Landing a sailboat at a mooring takes practice. Your goal is to stop your boat with the bow directly into the wind right up against the mooring, so that a crew member can take hold of the pendant and secure it to the bow. Moorings are always attached to a fitting through the bow and onto a cleat so the boat swings around it. If your boat sails past the mooring, do not try to hold on to it from the stern. Instead, let it go and sail around until you make a better landing. Once again practice is the key. When returning your boat to its mooring you should follow these steps:

1. Check that you are able to stay at the mooring.
2. If it is not already down, lower the centerboard to give you stability.

3. Lower and remove the jib.
4. Approach the mooring from downwind.
5. Pick up and secure the mooring line.
6. Lower and remove the mainsail.
7. Remove and stow the rudder and tiller.
8. Bail out the boat.
9. Double-check all the mooring lines.
10. Secure the halyards.
11. Put the sail bags and other gear away.
12. Replace the cockpit cover.

Ramps

In many parks, recreational facilities and clubs, boats are launched from large concrete ramps that go into the water. The boat is rolled down on a dolly until it is in the water. Launching from a ramp takes great care, since the part that is in the water often develops a large amount of slippery growth. Proceed down the ramp with caution. When launching a boat push it slowly into the water until it begins to float. Once the boat is floating, push it away from the dolly while a second person pulls the dolly out. Hold on to the boat. Never allow it to get away from you. Raise your sails and push off from the ramp. If there is an offshore breeze, you can simply sail away. However, if the breeze is onshore it may mean that you have to walk out a considerable distance to get the centerboard down, the rudder in and the mainsail up. This is normal procedure; don't let it worry you.

Be careful of ramps. They are slippery and are particularly dangerous around the edges because of deep water. With an onshore breeze the waves break close to the ramp, so it is important to get away as quickly as possible. Never get between the boat and shore when there are breaking waves.

When you are bringing the boat in, push the dolly into the water. Have the front of it pointing directly up the ramp so that when you bring your boat in the bow is pointing toward shore and can easily be pulled out. Your centerboard should be up, the sails down and the rudder out before you put the boat on the dolly. If you are lifting a boat out of the water, use three people, one on each side and one at the bow. If there are only two people it is best to have one on each side. If you do not have a dolly, you may find it helpful to have a set of life jackets ready to put the boat on when it comes out of the water. Whatever system you use, never leave your boat unattended. If you are beaching the boat without a ramp, have the sails down, the centerboard up and the rudder out before you get to the beach, and keep the boat outside the breaking waves until you are ready to lift it out. Watch for a smooth set of waves before taking it all the way in. Try to find a sandy part of the beach, one that is away from gravel. Never get between the hull of your boat and the shore because the surf can roll the boat over on top of you.

With larger boats, ramp launching demands backing a car down the ramp. Make sure your brakes are in good shape, and that the trailer is securely attached to the car. Special equipment and winches are needed for this type of operation, and it's best to check with local experts before proceeding the first time.

Man Overboard

"Man overboard" is a serious situation on all boats. Every second is valuable; time is of the essence until you have picked the person up.

First, throw a life jacket over the side to the person in the water; then assign someone to watch the person in the water. It is very important to keep him in sight; you can't waste valuable time searching. Shout "Man overboard" to the crew, so they understand why you are maneuvering.

If the accident occurs while you are sailing with the wind abeam or forward of abeam, jibe and approach the person in the water from the leeward side. The mainsail should be trimmed, then eased off to prevent the boom from slamming across the boat; you could injure someone or damage your rigging, thus compounding the situation.

If you are sailing before the wind when the accident occurs, bring the wind abeam and sail away for a few boat lengths. Then bring the boat about, reach back on the other tack and head into the wind. Or, continue sailing for a short distance and tack back. This should bring you to the person in the water on the second tack. Approach the person in the water slowly while spilling the wind from your sails. Keep your sheets loose so the boat is almost dead in the water. Be sure your centerboard is all the way down to ensure stability. When you are close to the person in the water, throw him a line and when he gets to the boat help him in over the stern.

If you fall overboard DO NOT PANIC; remain calm. Concentrate on keeping afloat the easiest way you can, using as little energy as possible. Make sure you stay clear of the rescue craft so you don't get hit by it. You're a better judge of how close it is to you than the skipper.

Be prepared to administer artificial respiration. Once the victim is back in the boat, quickly clear his mouth of any foreign matter. Tilt his head back so the chin is pointing upward. Open your mouth wide and place it tightly over his. Pinch the nostrils shut and blow into his mouth. Remove your mouth and allow the air to escape. Repeat until the victim starts breathing on his own.

In summary, follow these steps if there is a man overboard:

1. Throw in a life jacket.
2. Keep watch on the person in the water.
3. Shout "Man overboard."
4. Return as quickly as possible to pick up the person in the water.

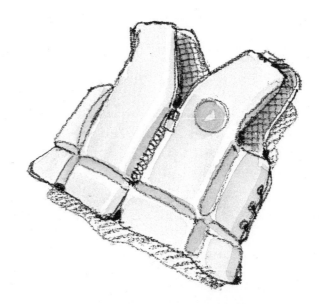

41. Life jackets must *be onboard for each and every crewmember.*

Rules of the Road

There are often situations on the water where there is a chance of a collision between two or more boats. There are rules to cover these situations. These are known as the right-of-way rules or Rules of the Road. Every sailor must follow these rules for his own safety and that of others. You may think that it is impossible for two boats to collide when they have the wide open spaces of water around them in which to maneuver. But it is all the open space which causes people to relax and be less vigilant.

When the helmsman and crew are sitting to windward, they are blind to boats approaching from leeward behind the sails. One crew member should be assigned to look to leeward occasionally to be sure the course is clear. If someone other than the skipper notices a boat in their course, he should immediately report its position to the skipper.

A decision is then made as to which boat is the "privileged vessel," the one with the right-of-way, and which is the "burdened vessel," the one that must stay clear.

There are several different water traffic rules. Which set will apply to you depends on where you sail. Most American sailors come under the jurisdiction of the Inland Rules of the Road, which apply to boats in bays and estuaries connected with the Atlantic or Pacific Oceans or the Gulf of Mexico. Such major boating areas as Long Island Sound, Chesapeake and Biscayne Bays, San Francisco Bay and Puget Sound are covered by the Inland Rules. In the ocean or the Gulf of Mexico, you are subject to the International Rules of the Road. The boundary between these two jurisdictions is an imaginary line drawn across the mouths of rivers, harbors, and inlets along the coasts. You can get a free copy of *U.S. Coast Guard Navigation Rules, International-Inland* (CG-169) by writing to the following address:

Commandant (G-WLE-4/73)
U.S. Coast Guard Headquarters
400 Seventh Street, S.W.
Washington, DC 20590

This publication lists the boundaries of the Inland and International jurisdictions in case you are in an area where there is some doubt.

Under the Inland Rules, when two sailboats encounter each other the following applies:

1. A boat that is running gives way to a boat that is close-hauled.

2. A boat on port tack gives way to one on starboard tack.

3. A boat to windward gives way to a boat to leeward of itself.

4. A boat overtaking another boat gives way to the slower boat.

It is important for the sailor to know the "order of ifs" under the Inland Rules:

1. If one boat is running and the other is close-hauled, the close-hauled boat must hold its course and speed while the running boat takes avoiding action.

2. If both vessels are close-hauled or running, but one of them is on port tack and the other is on starboard, then the boat on starboard stands on.

3. If both boats are running or close-hauled (or reaching) and both are on the same tack, then the boat which is to windward of the other must take avoiding action.

Under the International Rules, no distinction is made between a boat that is running and one that is close-hauled, and only two situations exist:

1. The starboard tack boat has right-of-way when two boats are on different tacks.

2. When both boats are on the same tack, the windward boat gives the right-of-way.

In general, sailboats have right-of-way over powerboats, but there are three exceptions:

1. When a sailboat is overtaking another boat, no matter how the other boat is propelled, the

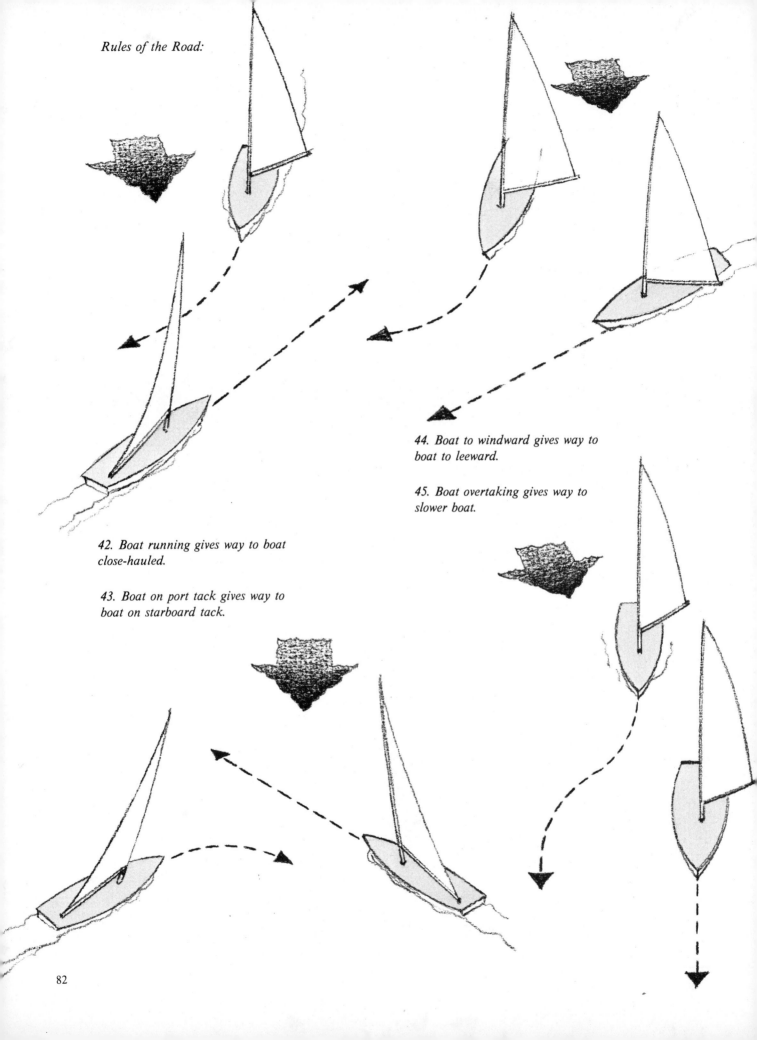

44. Boat to windward gives way to boat to leeward.

45. Boat overtaking gives way to slower boat.

42. Boat running gives way to boat close-hauled.

43. Boat on port tack gives way to boat on starboard tack.

sailboat is the "burdened vessel."

2. Commercial fishing vessels engaged in fishing with nets, lines or trawls must not be interfered with.

3. In a narrow channel or confined area, a sailboat must not hamper the safe passage of power-driven vessels which can navigate only inside such a channel or area.

A sailboat is only a sailboat when propelled by the wind alone. If the engine is going, it is a powerboat and must follow the powerboat rules of the road. The three basic right-of-way situations for powerboats are:

1. Two power boats approaching each other should pass port side to port side (give way to the right).

2. When two powerboats are crossing more or less at right angles, the boat on the right has the right-of-way.

3. When one powerboat is overtaking another, the overtaken boat has the right-of-way. The overtaking boat should pass to port.

Boats coming out of slips into the open, or leaving berths at piers and docks, have no rights until they are entirely clear.

When a powerboat alters course to give way to another vessel, the skipper should indicate his movements by signalling with his whistle or horn, as follows:

1. One short blast: "I am directing my course to starboard."

2. Two short blasts: "I am directing my course to port."

3. Three short blasts: "I am proceeding astern (in reverse)."

4. Four or more blasts: danger.

A good idea is to carry a spare can of Freon for the horn. Even better is to carry a combination air horn. When the air runs out, you can still use good old lung power.

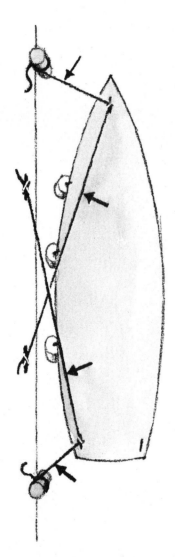

46. Dock lines. Bow and stern lines keep boat from moving from dock. Spring lines keep boat from surging backward and forward.

Lines and Their Uses

The proper use of mooring lines can simplify the docking and undocking of a boat and protect the boat during rough weather. Below are the lines necessary for docking a boat:

Bow lines: Inshore bow line—lead from an inshore chock to a cleat on the dock (see figure 46). Offshore bow line—lead through the offshore chock to a separate cleat on the dock.

Stern lines: Inshore stern line—lead from an inshore chock to a cleat on the dock (see figure 46). Offshore stern line—lead from an offshore cleat on the boat to a separate cleat on the dock. If this line is not employed, most boats will ride at their berths with the bow angled towards the dock and the stern angled away from the dock.

Spring line: The spring line is the most valuable line to employ when docking and undocking. When maneuvering away from a berth, a spring line should be led from the after end of the boat forward to a cleat on the dock. This is an after spring line. With all of the bow lines and the forward spring line let go, and the engine put slow astern, the bow will swing away from the dock.

Be familiar with the types of line and for what job each is best suited. The most common lines are listed below.

Manila is an all-purpose rope made in several

grades. The fibers have a natural protective lubrication but are usually treated with preservatives to resist rot and marine life. Manila is cheaper than synthetics but not as strong size for size. It must be kept as dry as possible for long life. It has some elasticity and is often used for mooring and anchor lines. The better grades are used for sheets, halyards, and other running rigging.

Cotton is soft, pliable, and easy to handle except when wet. Cotton lines are used mostly in small sizes for flag halyards and lanyards.

Nylon has superior strength (more than twice as strong as manila) as well as a stretch characteristic with high recovery quality. It is rot- and mildew-proof, easy to handle and highly resistant to abrasion. It is excellent for anchor and mooring lines, although it loses about 10 percent of its strength when wet.

Dacron retains its full strength when it is wet and has only slight stretch under loads. It is as strong as nylon with similar characteristics. It is used for sheets, halyards, and other running rigging.

Polyethylene is made in a variety of colors. It has twice the strength of manila and very little stretch. Its floatability makes it popular for ski tow ropes and dinghy painters. Polyethylene is adversely affected by heat and friction.

Polypropylene has a higher melting point than polyethylene, is more abrasive-resistant, and not as slippery. It is used for ski tow ropes and where low stretch is important.

Someone once said that if you can't tie good knots, tie plenty of them. This may be true, but the problem is that a badly tied knot significantly reduces the strength of a line and is also difficult to undo. These are thousands of knots and people spend lifetimes learning and inventing new ones.

The following knots are the basic ones that all seamen use. They are easy and can be learned in a short time.

Figure eight knot (see figure 47). The figure eight knot does not jam and is good to use as a "stop knot" to keep the ends of lines from running out through blocks.

Square knot (see figure 48). The square knot is probably the most useful knot known. The square knot is used for tying light lines together. Do not use the square knot to tie lines of different sizes together as it will slip. It is put to such numerous uses that many landlubbers call it the "sailor's knot." However, it jams and is difficult to untie after being heavily stressed.

Bowline (see figure 49). The bowline knot is second to the square knot in usefulness. It does not slip, jam or become difficult to untie. Bowlines are used wherever a secure loop or noose is needed in the end of a line. They are also used to secure lines to anchors when there is no time to make a splice.

You must also know how to secure a line to a cleat properly:

Half hitch (see figure 50). The half hitch, which completes the fastening, is taken with the free part of the line. The line can then be freed without taking up slack in the standing part. The line can't be freed without taking up slack in the standing part. Accidents have been caused by using this method of fastening on lines which must be freed quickly.

Clove hitch (see figure 51). The clove hitch is used for making a line temporarily fast to a piling.

Lines should never be left in a heap, whether on deck or in a locker. A line is always coiled so it will be ready in a hurry without kink or tangle. Coil a line down with the lay. To make a straight coil, a circular loop of the secured end is laid and successive loops are placed on top. It is especially

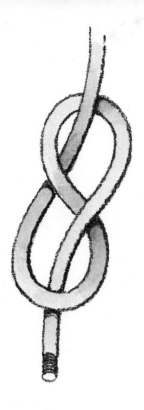

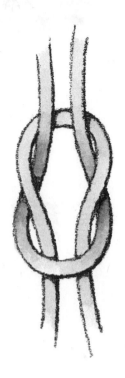

47. *Figure eight knot.*

48. *Square knot.*

49. *Bowline.*

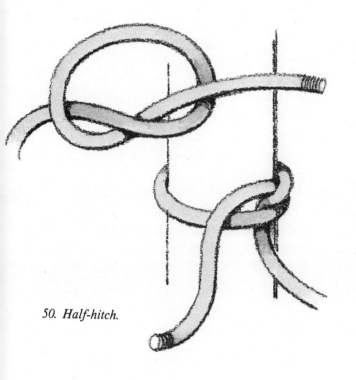

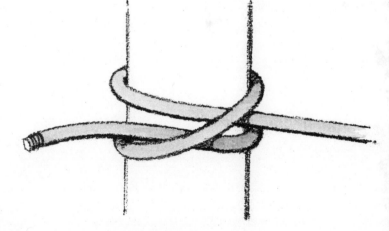

51. *Clove hitch.*

50. *Half-hitch.*

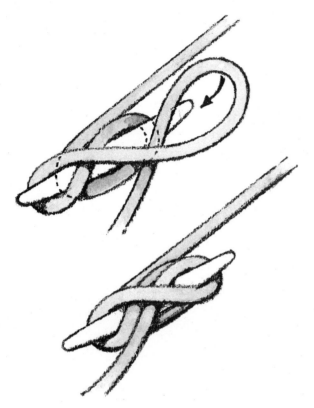

52. Cleating a line.

important to coil a line when it must be clear for running.

Cleat (see figure 52). Used for securing a line.

THE BOAT

The way people display pictures of their boats proves their love for sailing. The boat is really an extension of yourself; the boats people own reflect the people.

It is imperative to keep your boat in good shape. The maintenance of a sailboat requires a great deal of work; the bigger the boat, the more time spent keeping it up. For example, a 12-Meter sailboat requires five man-hours of work for every man-hour of sailing. Even a small boat like a Sunfish requires maintenance. Salt, sun and lack of care are the biggest factors leading to the decay of the boat. Boats should be washed with fresh water and kept out of the sun. All boats need to breathe; it is important to have inspection ports or breathing holes for fresh air to circulate under the decks and in the hull.

It is important to know your boat well: all of its parts, how they work and how to repair them if they break. Once you cast off from shore, your boat becomes a self-contained world. You can't afford to have breakdowns on the water. Learn the parts of your boat and their functions carefully. Go over them often so there is no question in your mind.

Parts of the Boat

Since you are trusting your boat to keep you afloat and get you safely to and from shore, you should have a thorough understanding of it and be familiar with its components. Don't let your fun be ruined by ignorance. Study the definitions below and refresh your memory as often as necessary.

1. Bailer: bucket or plastic container that can be used to get water out of a boat.

2. Battens: thin strips of wood or fiberglass which fit into pockets in the leech of the sail to give it support.

3. Block: a pulley rigged to act as a fairlead or to give a mechanical advantage.

4. Boom: a wood or metal pole used to extend the foot of a sail.

5. Boom vang: a pulley arrangement leading from the boom to the mast, used to hold the boom down.

6. Bow: the forward or front part of the boat.

7. Buoyancy tank: a water- and air-tight chamber to keep the boat afloat in case of swamping or capsizing.

8. Centerboard: a wooden or metal board carried in a trunk and lowered to overcome the sideways motion of the boat.

9. Centerboard pendant: the line or handle used to raise or lower the centerboard.

10. Cleat: a wooden or metal fitting with horns for securing lines.

53. A typical sheet lead block.

11. Cunningham: a line in the foot of the sail near the luff used for changing the draft of the sail.

12. Fairlead: an eye or block used to give a line a clear run or lead.

13. Forestay: a line or wire coming from the top of the mast to the bow, onto which the jib is hanked; it prevents the mast from falling backward.

14. Gooseneck: a swivel fitting that secures the boom to the mast and allows the boom to pivot around the mast.

15. Gunwale: the upper edge of the boat's side; the run-rail.

16. Halyards: lines used to hoist the sails.

17. Hiking straps: lines, webbing or slings under which the feet are hooked to increase leverage and prevent falling overboard when hiking out.

18. Hull: the portion of the boat comprised of the bottom, sides, buoyancy tanks, deck; the basic boat minus the rigging.

19. Jibsheets: two lines, one for each side, used for trimming or hauling in the jib.

20. Mainsheet: a single line, sometimes with both ends led clear, but generally with one end secured, used for trimming or hauling in the mainsail.

21. Mast: the vertical spar or pole that supports the sails and boom.

22. Outhaul: a line on the after end of the boom used to stretch out the foot of the sail.

23. Painter: a short line secured to the bow for making the boat fast.

24. Rudder: a flat shape, generally of wood, fitted onto the stern with pins and eyes and used to steer the boat.

25. Shackle: a U-shaped piece of steel, fitted with a pin that closes the opening, used for

securing blocks and eyes.

26. Shrouds: lines or wires from the masthead to the gunwales to keep the mast from swaying.

27. Stern: the after or back end of a boat.

28. Thwart: seat that extends from side to side.

29. Tiller: wood or metal arm attached to the top of the rudder and used to turn the rudder.

30. Tiller extension: a wood or metal pivoting extension attached to the tiller.

31. Transom: in boats having a flat board-like section at the stern, that section.

32. Traveller: a slide and car arrangement to which the lower end of the mainsheet purchase is attached, allowing it to be sheeted in more to one side or the other.

Equipment

Check your equipment to make sure your boat is ready. A well-equipped boat and crew is the start of safe sailing. The dangers of the water can easily be avoided by basic precautions that don't get in the way of having fun. It's a matter of careful planning. The following is a list of equipment that I recommend that you have on your boat:

1. A wearable Coast Guard-approved life jacket for each person. Coast Guard-approved jackets are comfortable to wear and come in several sizes. They are brightly colored so you can

easily spot a man overboard.

2. A strong tiller and hiking stick with a universal joint attaching the hiking stick to the tiller.

3. A rudder. Keep your rudder varnished so that water does not rot the wood and cause cracks. Check the pintels and gudgeons for rust and hidden cracks which could break while you're on the water. It is vital that the rudder and pintels attaching it to the boat be strong.

4. A centerboard with fittings. The centerboard should move easily up and down in the trunk.

5. An outhaul. An outhaul is used to pull the clew of the sail toward the end of the boom. Check that the lines are not frayed and it works easily.

6. A boom vang. Considerable force is put on the vang, particularly in waves when the boom rides up and down. Check the vang often for wear in the wire.

7. A mainsheet and fittings. The load on the mainsheet is distributed across the boom and is normally not particularly strong at any one point. Normal wear and tear, however, frays the line at specific blocks. Reverse the line to prolong the life of the mainsheet.

8. A sail and battens. Make sure the battens are all the way in the sail, so they do not work themselves out when the sail luffs. Check the batten pockets, as the cloth and stitching can rip.

9. A hiking strap. Be sure the hiking strap is strong and the lines are bolted through the deck so they will not pull out.

10. A downhaul. The downhaul should be led so it runs easily to adjust the luff of the sail.

11. A bailer. Every boat should have at least one bailer on board.

12. Lines. Each line should be used for only

one purpose. Carry spare lines for emergencies.

13. Paddles and oars. Every boat should have either a paddle or a set of oars in case the wind dies down.

14. A throwable flotation device. A cushion or life jacket should be available to throw to a man overboard. (See figure 54.)

15. A repair kit. Every boat should have a repair kit containing the following equipment:
- needle and line to sew sails
- screwdriver and pliers
- extra shackles
- extra small line
- sail tie lines
- silicone sealant

54. A horseshoe buoy is the best throwable flotation device.

Upkeep

To get the most out of your boat and sails, they must be properly maintained. Wash your boat down every time you come back from sailing. Salt can do a lot of damage to your boat's finish if it is left to work on it. Replace broken parts so that your boat is always in optimum working order. Be sure to store your boat properly. If you keep it on land, store it hull up to preserve the shape. If you keep it in a berth, tie it properly to avoid damage from rough weather. Use covers to keep out water and leaves, etc.

Your sails also require care. Use sail covers if you roll your mainsail on the boom, or a roller furling jib, as synthetic sails are affected by long exposure to sunlight.

Use sail bags if you have them. Fold your sails smoothly to avoid wrinkling. In light air an uneven surface will cause turbulence in the flow of air across the sail. The proper sail folding procedure is as follows:

1. Spread the sail flat with the foot into the wind.

2. Fold the sail accordian-style from the foot to the head, making the width of each fold slightly shorter than the length of the sail bag. Continue folding until the entire sail is folded. If the sail has a plastic window, first fold the foot of the sail over it. Do not fold the window.

3. Fold over the ends.

4. Without pressing hard, roll or fold the sail into a rectangular shape to fit the sail bag. Avoid stuffing, which causes creases and loss of shape.

5. Slide the folded sail into the bag.

When washing salt from your sails, use fresh water so they will dry properly. Never allow sails to flap in heavy wind; this weakens the fabric. Only hoist the sails to their design limits between the black bands on the mast.

Boating Etiquette

Sailing is more enjoyable for everyone when basic good manners are observed. Below are some fundamental rules of boating etiquette:

1. Do not jettison garbage.

2. Arrange your mooring before landing; this is easily done by a phone call before setting sail or by hailing people on shore.

3. Avoid tying up to government buoys or navigational aids.

4. Anchor in areas that are clear of traffic and away from narrow channels. Many harbors have specific anchorage areas marked by special buoys.

5. Follow the right-of-way rules.

6. Stay clear of boats with fishing lines.

7. Ask permission from the owner or skipper before boarding another boat.

8. Always offer assistance to a boat in distress.

9. Anchor with plenty of room away from other anchored boats.

10. When crewing on someone else's boat it is best not to offer unsolicited advice.

55. *Always bag trash securely and dispose ashore.*

Giving and Taking Orders

It is as difficult to give an order as it is to take it. As a skipper, be tactful when giving an order; as a crew member, be willing and able to obey all reasonable commands. Remember, Stonewall Jackson once said, "Obedience to orders, instant and unhesitating, is not only the life blood of armies and navies but the security of states." On pleasure boats just as on military vessels, the skipper is in charge and each crew member has specific responsibilities.

Give orders in a friendly but firm tone of voice. Don't shout. It only makes the crew nervous and induces mistakes. Explain things in advance to inexperienced crew members so they feel more relaxed. Give commands in exact terms. For example, ask for sails to be trimmed in four inches instead of "a little." By putting commands exactly there is no doubt as to what you want. The best skippers are those that ask the advice of the rest of the crew. However, in times of quick action the crew must obey commands immediately and ask questions later.

A skipper can delegate authority but never responsibility. It is the captain who calls the shots and the captain who goes down with the ship.

Selecting a Boat

There are many options to choose from in deciding on a boat. Make a list of questions to ask yourself. How do you plan to use your boat? Will it be for day sailing or longer cruises? Do you wish to do some racing? Will you stow your boat on a trailer? Do you want a single-handed boat or a boat for two or more people? Where you sail is also important. Are you in shallow or warm waters? Will you sail in the North when it is cold? If you sail in shallow waters, you will want a centerboard or shoal draft boat that doesn't draw much water. You may be in an area with a low bridge and need to be able to take the mast down. You may be sailing off a beach. Of course, the overriding question is: can you afford a boat? I believe you should buy a boat that you can outfit and sail well and still afford. It is better to have a smaller boat with first class equipment than to stretch and have a boat that puts you over your budget.

Before buying a boat, think about where you will keep it. If you get a larger day sailer or cruising boat, you may have to keep it in a marina. In many places marinas are overcrowded and expensive. You may have to rent a slip at a marina that is a considerable distance from your home.

When you buy a boat, it is better to take the options offered even if it makes the price higher, because the boat will last longer, retain more value, and be better to sail.

Many sailors charter a boat similar to the one they are considering for a period of time to see how they like it. A used boat is often a good buy. Buying a used boat can be like buying a used car; you are never sure what shape it is in. However, if the boat does have problems, they usually have been corrected by the previous owner. A used boat often has more options on it than a new boat, and you may get a good break on the price. As a rule, sailboats, particularly cruising and day sailers, retain a good part of their value. Buying a used boat can have disadvantages; you may be buying someone else's trouble. It is helpful, particularly on larger boats, to have a survey of the boat done by an expert so you know exactly what shape it is in. It is often best to buy a boat through an experienced broker or dealer.

Probably the best way I know of to select a boat is to try out several and then go to a boat show. There are more than 300 boat shows every year held in all parts of the country where every size and shape of boat on the market is displayed. While at the show you can pick up a company's literature and talk to its representatives. Make a list of what you require in a boat and then talk with each company's people; don't buy until you have considered every point. Even then it may be better to test the boat for a weekend first.

If you buy a new boat and find that it leaks, return it immediately. The sooner you have discrepancies taken care of by the builder, the better off you will be. Most new boats have a warranty, and the seller of the used boat will feel responsible to make sure you have gotten what you paid for. However, it is up to you to insist. Statistics show that the average boat owner will trade or buy a new boat between three and four years after buying the first.

Trailers

Many sailors use trailers to store their boats. This is the most versatile form of boat storage, and lets you sail on a different body of water every weekend. You can store the boat in your driveway, which eliminates storage costs and the chance of vandalism.

There are two types of trailers. The boom variety emphasizes keel support; the frame type emphasizes hull support. Select a trailer that will keep your boat from losing its shape. The trailer should meet local and state trailer regulations, permit dry launching, and provide maximum safety and comfort while being towed.

When pulling your boat and trailer there are a few things you should keep in mind. Be sure your equipment rides well without shifting, chafing, and rattling. Balance is very important when trailering. Too much weight in the rear of the boat will cause your trailer to bob.

Don't forget that you are really driving two vehicles, not one. Travel a little slower than normal and allow plenty of room to brake. An outside rearview mirror is very helpful and lights on the rear of the trailer are a must.

Once you get to your launching ramp or beach, the hints below will help you launch your boat.

When launching your boat from a sandy beach, deflate your tires a little, as this will improve traction. Leaving from a beach is simplified by using an outboard motor.

When backing into the water, come into the shoreline at right angles. Remember that to turn your trailer to the right, turn the wheel to the left. To turn the trailer to the left, turn the wheel to the right.

Before you launch the boat from the trailer, step the mast in place and attach the rigging and sails. Don't hoist the sails until you're in the water.

You may decide to keep your boat at a marina. They usually have launching ramps or a hoist, dinghy service, docks, and a clubhouse with lockers and showers. Or, you might choose to keep it at a yacht club. They don't usually offer as much as marinas but will have docks, a clubhouse and probably swimming and sailing lessons. Yacht clubs get more into the social aspects of sailing. They can also be appreciably cheaper than marinas. You pays your money, and takes your choice.

Special Boats

There are some principles of sailing that apply equally to a Sunfish or a 12-Meter yacht. Mastering one helps to master the other.

In the past few years there has been a huge growth in windsurfers, catamarans, and small cruising boats. The trend is away from small dinghies that capsize and are not self-righting toward easier-to-handle self-righting boats. Generally, the larger the boat the easier it is to handle and the more forgiving it is. Smaller boats are harder to handle since they are relatively unstable and capsize following the simplest mistake. It is important to get a foundation in dinghy sailing before moving up. The best large boat sailors are the ones who learned on small boats first.

WINDSURFING

Learning to sail a Windsurfer can be very enjoyable or extremely frustrating. To have a successful first attempt at windsurfing it is necessary to have ideal conditions, beneficial to have the use of some type of training equipment and helpful if you have some good instruction.

Conditions

Under ideal conditions, the wind is less than 8 knots and the seas are calm. The area in which you sail should be relatively free of boat traffic and obstructions. The smaller the area the better, so long as the breeze is not excessively obstructed by buildings.

Equipment

The basic and most common training windsurfer for a beginner has a smaller sail. A training sail is usually around 43 square feet (stock sails are 56 square feet). A smaller sail takes a lot of the power out of the rig and reduces the tendency for the beginner to get over-powered. The ideal piece of training equipment is the specially designed Windsurfer Star, manufactured by Windsurfing International. The board is wider and stable and the rig (booms and mast) is made of aluminum and fiberglass. This makes it easier to pull the rig out of the water and hold it on center.

Instruction

Qualified instruction is available around the world through International Windsurfer Sailing Schools. Headquarters are at the following address: 1038 Princeton Drive, Marina Del Rey, CA 90291. The instructional program consists of two three-hour lessons. Certified instructors teach the classes using special equipment. Classes start with background material on the sport and sailing theory. The instructor demonstrates each step of windsurfing on a hydraulic land simulator, and each student then practices the steps. The instructor corrects the student's mistakes on land, before he goes onto the water, thus saving a lot of time. Later, students use the Windsurfer Star and regular Windsurfers with training-sized sails.

Windsurfing Step-by-Step

There is no substitute for good instruction in windsurfing. However, the steps listed below will help you get an idea of what it's all about.

Getting ready. Establish the wind direction and aim the board crosswise to the wind. Point the mast straight downwind, so that the mast and the board form a right angle.

Stance. Face the sail with your back to the wind. Place your feet on the center line of the board. The forward foot should be in front of the mast and the back foot over the daggerboard. Keep your feet centered unless tacking or jibing. Straighten your back and keep your hips forward.

Getting started. Be sure the board is crosswise to the wind. Pull the mast straight up out of the water. To do this, hold the uphaul with both hands, reach across with your forward hand (the one closest to the front), and grab the boom about six inches from the end. Next, pull up the mast, using your forward hand, until it is close to your forward leg. Reach back with your back hand and grab the boom. To fill the sail with wind, pull in with your back hand. At the same time, tip the mast and sail towards the nose of the board to keep it from rounding up into the wind.

Control. Hold the rig out of the water by the uphaul. To turn the board away from the wind, tip the mast forward and pull in with the back hand. To turn the board up into the wind, tip the mast back and let out with the back hand. Keep the mast in the center plane. Remember, your

body weight and the sail control the board.

Turning. The sail is used to tack or jibe. To tack, lean the luffing sail back and step around to the front of the board as it turns into the wind. Stand on the bow of the board with a foot on either side of the center as the sail luffs over the stern. Lean the sail to the left or right to complete the 180° turn. As the turn completes, step back to the center line of the board.

To jibe, lean the sail forward. As the board turns down wind, step around to the back of it. Stand on the stern of the board as the sail luffs over the bow. Lean the sail to the left or right to complete the turn. As board moves crosswise to the wind, step back to the center line.

Tips. If you become over-powered, release the boom with your back hand. This will let the wind out of the sail just as a mainsheet would. If you release the boom with your forward hand, the board will react as if you had cut a shroud.

It is important to keep your feet on the center line. To gain balance, bend at the knees and use the sail. If over-powered, let out the sail; if falling backwards, pull in with your back hand to catch more wind.

Advanced technique. Sailing in stronger winds requires some experience. In high winds you must hang from the boom out over the water and use your body weight to its utmost. This means you will grip the boom further back and keep your feet much further back on the board. In extreme winds it is necessary to change daggerboards. Use high-wind daggerboards to reduce the planing surface and move the center of lateral resistance aft when the winds are over 15 knots. Since the high-wind daggerboard is smaller and swept back, it reduces the board's tendency to round up into the wind, and makes it possible to bear off and surf on the waves in a strong wind.

CATAMARANS

Catamarans have two hulls of equal length, with the mast supported in the center of the bridge deck between them. Some designs have flexible connections between the hulls and all accommodations in the hulls, and some designs have large bridge deck structures with no accommodations at all in the hulls. Smaller day-racing catamarans are generally grouped into several additional groups. These include boats whose only function is high speed and maximum performance. In that group fall boats like the Toronado, which has semi-rounded hulls, pivoting centerboards and a fully articulating mast with fully battened mainsail. This group also includes "C" class catamarans. These are the most sophisticated sailboats in existence and also the most close-winded boats afloat. "C" class catamarans are easily identified by their wing masts and airplane-like structure. Finally, there is a group of day-racing catamarans which might be called beach boats. These boats, such as the Hobie 14, the Hobie 16, and the various sizes of Prindles, have no daggerboards, but have asymmetrical hulls which get their lift to windward in the same way the sails do. These cats are designed for spirited performance and high speed, and are geared toward beachability, rugged use and recreational activity. With minimum camping gear, some hearty folks even go cruising in them.

Trimarans

Trimarans have three hulls; beyond that, there is little that is standard. The length of the outer hulls, spacing from the main hulls, percentage of buoyancy, shape, etc., vary a great deal. There are very few day-sailing trimarans, since the technology is not practical on boats under 25 feet.

Trimarans do have one advantage over cats: they warn you of impending capsize by burying the leeward *ama* or hull, giving you time to luff-up or let out the main.

Why a Catamaran?

The first advantage in catamaran sailing is absolute, blinding speed; no vessel can compare with the potential speed of a catamaran. The second advantage of a catamaran is its great stability. It is easy to board and to disembark. It's an easy boat to rig, and you can walk around on it without tipping it over. It is also easy to beach, easy to trailer, and much lighter than many of its single-hulled counterparts.

Handling

There are some handling differences between catamarans and most single-hulled boats. The chief difference with the majority of designs is in tacking. Most catamarans, because of their extremely light weight, have no momentum to carry them through a tack and must be backwinded. In many cases it is necessary to backwind the jib to bring the boat completely around onto the other tack. (The secret is to not release the jib sheet until the main has filled on the new tack.) In a racing situation this means that the short tacking that might be done with a very nimble monohull vessel will probably be a disastrous tactic with a catamaran. In catamaran racing, try to do as few tacks as possible because of the loss of time involved.

The next item of catamaran handling to be considered is learning to sail the boat flat. Catamarans are designed to sail with both hulls in the water or with the windward hull just kissing the water. Hot-dogging, or "flying a hull," is a lot of fun and very exciting, but detrimental to the performance of the boat.

Keeping the boat flat is an acquired skill; it is mostly done with the tiller. In airs that are too heavy for the tiller alone, it is done by easing the traveller and sometimes easing the mainsheet. The secret of keeping the boat flat is to turn downwind when the hull begins to rise. If you turn upwind, unless you are "pinching," the forces that are lifting the hull in the first place will accelerate. A basic difference in handling a catamaran as opposed to a single-hulled boat is turning downwind when the boat becomes over-pressed, rather than turning upwind and letting the boat luff. This is because in a single-hulled boat the additional momentum gained by turning upwind heels the boat a little further, allowing the rig to spill the wind. In a catamaran, the same forces apply. However, if the boat heels further, the threat of capsize becomes greater; and since you are trying to bring the hull back down to the water, you must turn downwind rather than up.

A catamaran sailor seldom sails directly downwind because downwind sailing is the slowest point of sail. When sailing dead downwind, a boat can achieve only a percentage of the true wind speed. However, tacking downwind increases speed enormously. Therefore, the most frequently used procedure with a catamaran is to reach toward the mark and turn downwind until you are getting less drive out of the sails. When you reach this point, head back up slightly and maintain that course. Find the best possible course downwind, until your sails are full and drawing and deriving their maximum power without actually going downwind. This is often about 15 degrees to either side of the true wind. A simple jibe brings you on to the other tack. Tack downwind in the same manner that you tack upwind toward the mark. If you have boards, raise them fully to take advantage of your leeway.

Occasionally, you may be over-powered going downwind. In smaller boats this usually becomes apparent at about 20 to 25 knots of true wind speed. It is very important that you maintain your control over the boat at this time as extraordinary speeds can be achieved. In an emergency over-powering situation, the simplest and safest procedure is to fall off until you are going dead downwind. Haul your traveller in to the center, tighten the mainsheet, and try to feather the mainsail into the wind as you go downwind. Your fully battened sail will assist you in this. When you are going dead downwind, and the mainsheet is in as tight as possible, the traveller centered, and you are ready, release your halyard and pull your mainsail down as quickly as possible. Try to have your mast rotator straight with the sail during this operation so there is no chance of the sail jamming in the sail groove.

Rigs

Most modern catamarans have a fractional rig with a rotating mast and a fully battened mainsail. The high speed of the catamaran can take full advantage of this technology. The purpose of the rotating mast is to form a better air foil with the sail. The mast is rotated in such a way that the windward side of the mast is a continuous line with the windward side of the sail. The mast rotator combined with the fully battened sail allows you to change the camber in the sail to match the wind strength. As with any boat, the stronger the wind the less camber is needed. When sailing a catamaran it will be possible to change the camber of the sail depending on your apparent wind, because the apparent wind will change rapidly even though the true wind remains steady.

Capsize

Capsize on a catamaran is handled much the same as capsize on any other centerboard or non-ballasted boat. Swim the boat around so the sails face into the wind. Tie a righting line to the shroud on the windward hull. (If you don't have a righting line on board, undo the mainsheet from the block system and use it instead.) Be sure to release the mainsheet and jibsheet so the sails won't hold water, which makes righting more difficult; if the sails are left sheeted, the boat may sail away without you when it comes up. Where you stand on the hull as you rotate the boat back out of the water will depend on the type of boat. On some boats with daggerboards you can stand on the board to get more leverage. On some boats you can't; it is best to know before you get in this situation. Lean out against your righting line as far as possible to provide leverage to right the boat. When the boat begins to right and come over you, duck in between the hulls for maximum safety. Do not drop the righting line until you are aboard, as there is always a possibility the boat may sail away without you. Make sure the sheets don't make fast to anything until you're aboard . . . or you may have to go through the whole operation again.

Jibing

The broad base, stability, efficient traveller system, and lack of a permanent backstay allow a catamaran to be jibed simply and easily. When jibing in unusually heavy conditions, assist the rig in the jibe in order to take some strain off the equipment. In moderate airs, tighten the mainsheet before jibing, then push your tiller to windward and at moderate speed complete your jibe, allowing the traveller to swing across on the new tack by itself. In heavy airs, tighten the mainsheet, then assist the rig across the stern by hauling the traveller to center and then allowing it to pay out slowly on the opposite tack.

Apparent Wind

Apparent wind in catamaran sailing is most usual from forward of abeam. Since catamarans normally achieve a much higher percentage of the true wind speed than other boats, the apparent wind is normally much further forward. It is not unusual to see single-hulled boats and catamarans on the same course with the catamarans trimmed

in much closer than the single-hulled boats. Because the catamarans are moving faster, the apparent wind is further forward; since sails are trimmed to the apparent wind, the sails will be sheeted in tighter. The traveller on a catamaran is more important in controlling the sail than it is on many other classes of boat. Most champion catamaran sailors trim their mainsail to the proper shape for the wind speed and direction and then use the traveller to obtain the optimum angle of attack as they sail. As they accelerate they haul their travellers in toward the center line; as they decelerate they let the traveller out to maintain the same angle of attack. This is easy to achieve on a catamaran because of its very wide sheeting base and stability.

Glossary

A

Abaft. Toward the stern.
Abeam. At right angles to the centerline of a boat.
Aboard. On or in a boat.
Aft. Toward the stern.
Aground. When the hull or keel of a boat touches the bottom.
Aloft. Overhead, above the deck.
Amidships. Between fore and aft; the middle of the boat.
Anchor. A device shaped so as to grip the bottom. It is secured by a line from the boat.
Astern. Behind a boat; in the direction of the stern.
Athwartships. Across the beam of a boat; at right angles to the centerline.
Awash. Immersed in water.

B

Backstay. A wire support from the mast to the stern of the boat.
Bail. To remove water from the boat.
Ballast. Weight placed in the bottom of the boat on the keel to give it stability.
Bare Poles. With all sails down.
Battens. Thin wooden or plastic strips placed in pockets in the leech of a sail to help hold its form.
Beam. The width of a boat at its widest point.
Beam Wind. A wind which blows athwart a boat's centerline.
Bearing. The direction of an object.
Beat. To sail to windward.
Belay. To make fast a line to a cleat.
Bend. To secure or to make fast a sail to a spar. Also the knot by which one rope is made fast to another.
Bight. Loop.
Bilge. The interior of the hull below the floorboards.
Block. A nautical pulley.
Boat Hook. A device for catching hold of a ring bolt or line when coming alongside a pier or picking up a mooring.
Bolt Rope. Line stitched to the foot and luff of a sail.
Boom. The spar to which the foot of the sail is attached with lacing, slides, or in a groove.
Bow. Forward part of the boat.
Bowsprit. A spar extending forward from the bow.
Breastline. Mooring line leading roughly at right angles from the boat's sides.

Bridle. Rope span with ends secured for a sheet block to ride on.

Broach. To spin out of control and capsize or come close to it; loss of steering control.

Buoy. Any floating object anchored in one place to show position.

Burdened Vessel. A boat required to keep clear of a vessel holding the right of way.

C

Capsize. To tip over.

Careen. To place a boat on her side so that work may be carried out on her underwater parts.

Carry Away. To break or tear loose.

Cast Off. To let go of a line when leaving the dock or mooring.

Catboat. A sailboat with a single fore and aft sail.

Centerboard. A shaped blade attached to the underside of the hull to give the boat lateral resistance when it is sailing to windward; adjustable keel.

Chafe. To damage by rubbing.

Chain Plates. Metal plates bolted to the side of a boat to which shrouds are attached to support the rigging.

Chock. A fairlead for mooring or anchor lines.

Claw Off. To beat away from a lee shore.

Cleat. A fitting used to secure a line under strain.

Clew. The aft corner of a sail.

Close-Hauled. Sailing close to the wind; when the wind is well forward of abeam (90 degrees).

Close-Winded. Describes a craft capable of sailing very close to the wind.

Coaming. The raised protection around a cockpit.

Cockpit. The space at a lower level than the deck in which the tiller or wheel is located.

Cringle. A metal ring worked into the sail.

Crutch. Support for the boom when the sails are furled.

D

Displacement. The weight of water displaced by a boat.

Downhaul. Line attached to the tack of the sail and used to trim the draft forward.

Draft. The depth or fullness in a sail; the depth of the keel or centerboard in the water.

Drift. The leeway of a boat.

Dry Sailing. Keeping a boat out of water when not in use.

E

Ease. To let out.

F

Fairlead. A fitting used to change the direction of a line, giving it a better angle from a sail or block to a winch or cleat.

Fall. The part of a tackle to which the power is applied in hoisting.

Fathom. A nautical measurement for the depth of water. One fathom is equal to 6 feet.

Fetch. When a craft sailing to windward can make her objective without making another tack.

Foot. The bottom part of a sail.

Fore-and-Aft. In the direction of the keel, from front to back.

Foremast. Forward mast of a sailboat having two or more masts.

Forefoot. The forward part of the keel, adjoining the lower part of the stem.

Foul. Entangled or clogged.

Frames. Skeleton of a ship.

Free. Whenever you're not sailing close-hauled.

Freeboard. The distance from the gunwale to the waterline.

Full-and-By. Sailing as close to the wind as possible.

G

Gaff. A pole extending from a mast to support the head of a sail.

Gasket. A piece of rope or canvas used to secure a furled sail.

Gear. Any equipment pertaining to a sailboat.

Genoa. An overlapping headsail.

Gimbal. A device used for suspending the compass so it remains level.

Gooseneck. A device that secures the boom to the mast.

Grommet. A metal ring fastened in a sail.

Ground Tackle. Anchor, cable, etc. used to secure a boat.

Gudgeon. A fitting attached to the hull into which the rudder's pintels are inserted.

Gunwale. The rail of the boat at deck level.

Guy. A line or wire used to trim the spinnaker pole.

H

Halyard. A line used to haul sails up and down the mast.

Hard-a-Lee. The command to inform the crew to be prepared for a tack: helm is being pushed hard to leeward, turning the boat into the wind.

Head. Top of a sail.

Head-to-Wind. Condition where the bow is headed into the wind and the sails are shaking.

Headsails. Any sail used forward of the mast.

Headstay. A forward stay supporting the mast.

Headway. Moving ahead.

Heave. To position a boat's bow to the wind and hold it there (after which she is hove to).

Helm. A tiller or wheel.

Hike. To lean over the side of a boat to help counterbalance

heeling.
Hoist. The vertical edge of a sail; to hoist is to haul aloft.
Hull. The main body of the boat.

I

Inboard. Toward the centerline of the boat.
Irons. A boat is "in irons" when she is in the wind's eye and, having lost all headway, will not go off on either tack.
In Stays. When a boat is in the wind's eye while going from one tack to another.

J

Jib. Triangular sail set forward of the mainmast.
Jibe. A boat begins to jibe at the moment when, with the wind aft, the foot of her mainsail crosses her centerline. The boat completes the jibe when the mainsail has filled on the new tack.
Jibstay. A wire supporting the mast to which the luff of the jib is attached.
Jumper. This is a stay on the upper forward part of the mast.

K

Keel. A heavy fin under the hull. It prevents the boat from sideslipping by resisting the lateral force of the wind.
Ketch. A two-masted sailing vessel with smaller aftermast stepped forward of the sternpost.
Knee. A timber with two arms connecting frames and beams to give added strength.
Knot. A nautical unit of speed—6,080 feet or one nautical mile per hour.

L

Lanyard. A line fastened to an article, such as a pail, whistle, knife, or other small tool for purposes of securing it.
Lay. The twist of a rope's strands.
Lazarette. A small space below deck, aft of the cockpit, where spare parts are kept.
Leech. The after edge of a sail.
Leeward. Away from the wind.
Light Sails. Sails made of a light material for use in light winds.
List. A boat is said to list when it is leaning at an angle due to excess weight on one side.
Locker. A storage compartment on a boat.
Luff. 1. The forward vertical edge of a sail. 2. To alter course toward the wind until the boat is head to wind. 3. The flapping of a sail caused by the boat being head-to-wind.

M

Mainmast. The principal mast of a sailboat.

Mainsail. The sail set abaft the mainmast.
Mainsheet. The line for controlling the main boom.
Mizzen. The shorter mast aft on a yawl or ketch.
Mooring. A heavy anchor or weight permanently in position.
Mooring Buoy. A buoy fitted with a ring and used for mooring a boat.

N

Nun Buoy. A buoy with a conical top found on the starboard hand on entering a channel and painted red.

O

Offshore. Away from the shore.
Off the Wind. Sailing downwind or before the wind.
On the Wind. To sail close-hauled.
Outboard. Away from the centerline of the boat.
Outhaul. The line which pulls the mainsail away from the mast and tightens the foot of the sail along the boom.
Overstand. To sail past the lay line of a mark.

P

Painter. A short piece of rope secured in the bow of a small boat and used for making her fast.
Pay Off. To turn the bow away from the wind.
Peak. The upper after corner of a gaff sail.
Pennant. A three-sided flag.
Pinch. To sail so close to the wind as to allow the sails to shiver.
Pintle. A bolt of metal secured to the rudder and fitting into the gudgeon—gives a swinging support to the rudder.
Point. To head close to the wind.
Port. The left side of a boat when looking forward.
Privileged Vessel. One which has the right of way.

Q

Quarter. That portion of a vessel's sides near the stern.

R

Rail. The outer edge of the deck.
Rake. The angle of a boat's mast from the vertical.
Reach. Sailing with a beam wind.
"Ready About." An order to prepare for coming about.
Reef. To reduce the area of a sail by making fast reef points and earings.
Rib. An athwartship frame of a vessel.
Rig. A general description of a boat's upper works; to set up spars and standing and running rigging of a sailboat.
Rigging. Ropes securing masts and sails.
Roach. The curve of the afteredge of the mainsail.
Rudder. A steering device at the stern of the boat.

Run. Point of sailing when the wind is aft.

S

Scull. To move the rudder rapidly back and forth so as to propel the boat forward.

Seaway. Area with rough or moderate sea running.

Secure. To make safe.

Set. The direction of the leeway of a vessel, or of tide or current.

Shackle. A U-shaped piece of steel with eyes in the ends, closed by a shackle pin.

Shake Out. To let out a reef and hoist the sail.

Sheave. The wheel of a block over which the rope passes.

Sheet. The line used to control the forward or athwartships movement of a sail.

Shrouds. Wires that hold the mast upright at the sides.

Skeg. The continuation of the keel aft, protecting the propeller and sometimes taking the heel of the rudder.

Spinnaker. Balloonlike sail used on leeward legs.

Splice. To join rope by tucking the strands together.

Spreader. Support that keeps the shrouds away from the mast for better mast-bend control.

Squall. 1. A brief storm that arrives suddenly. 2. A prolonged gust of wind.

Starboard. The right side of a boat as one faces forward.

Standing Rigging. That part of a ship's rigging that is permanently secured and not moveable; e.g., stays, shrouds.

Starboard Tack. Sailing with the wind coming from the right side; sails on port side.

Stays. Wires supporting a mast in a fore and aft direction.

Staysail. A small triangular sail used forward of the mast on reaching legs.

Stem. The timber at the extreme forward part of a boat secured to the forward end of the keel and supporting the bow planks.

Step. The frame on the keelson into which the heel of a mast fits or steps.

Stern. The after section of the boat.

Stow. To put away.

Strake. A row of planks in the hull.

Swamp. To fill with water.

T

Tack. 1. The forward lower corner of a sail, where the luff and foot meet. 2. Point of sailing when the boat is heading to windward. 3. To change course by passing into the wind. A boat is tacking from the time she is beyond head-to-wind until she has assumed a close-hauled course, if sailing to windward. If she is not sailing to windward, the tack is completed when her mainsail fills on the new course.

Tackle. An arrangement of ropes and blocks to give a mechanical advantage.

Tender. A small boat employed to go back and forth to the shore from a larger boat.

Thimble. A ring grooved on the outside for a rope grommet.

Thwart. The athwartships seat in a boat.

Tiller. Steering lever that controls the rudder.

Topping Lift. A line from the mast to the spinnaker pole, controlling pole height and the draft position of the spinnaker—pole down, draft forward; pole up, draft aft.

Topside. On deck.

Transom. The stern of the hull.

Traveller. A sliding fitting to which the mainsheet is attached, keeping the boom in the same plane as it is moved in and out.

Trim. To adjust the sails.

Tuning. The delicate adjustment of a boat's rigging, sails, and hull to the proper balance which assures the best sailing performance.

Turnbuckle. A threaded link which pulls two eyes together for setting up standing rigging.

U

Unfurl. To cast loose a sail by throwing off the gaskets.

V

Vang. A line to steady the boom when off the wind.

Veer. A change of direction, as in the wind.

W

Wake. The waves from a boat.

Waterline. An imaginary line around the hull at the surface when the boat is on an even keel.

Weather. The state of the atmosphere at a certain time and place.

Well-Found. Well-equipped.

Whipping. To bind the strands of a line's end with yarn or cord.

Whisker Pole. A light spar extending from the mast and used to hold the jib out when sailing off the wind.

Winch. A mechanical device to aid in pulling a line. It consists basically of a drum, on which the line is wound, and a crank, to do the winding.

Windward. Toward the wind; opposite of leeward.

Wing-and-Wing. Running before the wind with the sails set on opposite sides.

Working Sails. Mainsail and working jib.

Y

Yacht. General term for a boat used solely for the personal pleasure of the owner.

Yaw. To steer wildly or out of the line of the course, as when running with a heavy quartering sea.

Checklist

Below is a checklist of equipment and procedures. It's a good idea to go down the list each time you go sailing, to make sure you haven't forgotten anything which might affect your safety or pleasure on the water. Space has been allowed to make notes or additions within each area of inspection.

Launching:

_____ Is everything on board secure?

_____ Are flotation compartments sealed?

_____ Do self-bailers work freely?

_____ Is all the rigging—standing and running—sorted out?

_____ Are bagged sails aboard?

_____ Are battens with the mainsail?

_____ Are life jackets stowed where easily accessible?

_____ Are rudder and centerboard attached to the boat with lanyards?

_____ Is the boat centered and secure aboard its dolly or trailer?

Make sure everything you'll need is aboard before casting-off. (Obvious, but we all forget things.) Here's what I need:

_____ Tools (screwdriver, pliers, knife and marlinspike)

_____ Extra blocks

_____ Spare shackles

_____ Spare line (small diameter)

_____ Silicone sealant

_____ Anchor and rode

_____ Flashlight

_____ Food

_____ Water

_____ Foul weather gear

_____ Sunglasses

_____ Sweater

_____ Hat

_____ Horn or whistle

_____ Throwable flotation device

_____ Paddle or oars

_____ Boat bailer

If all the above is ok, let's set sail:

_____ Are halyards untangled and free-running?

_____ Bend on the main. Are battens securely in their pockets?

_____ Are shackles tightly fastened?

_____ Is mainsheet slacked-off?

_____ Is the topping-lift attached?

_____ Next, hank on the jib, starting with the tack and working your way to the head. Make sure there's no fouling or twist.

_____ Shackle on the halyard.

_____ Bend on the sheets and run them back through the fairleads or blocks to the cockpit. Tie figure eight knots in the ends.

_____ Hoist the main.

_____ Hoist the jib.

_____ Cast-off and good sailing!

After returning to the dock or mooring, rinse the boat down with fresh water. Fold and bag the sails. Coil lines. Secure everything on board. Come the end of the season, it's time to put things in order for the long, cold winter.

_____ Take the sails to your sailmaker for cleaning and repairs.

_____ Scrub down the boat with fresh water.

_____ Apply a light coating of WD-40 or similar lubricant to all metal fittings.

_____ Tie the standing rigging to the mast.

_____ Store the mast on its side, well supported along its length.

_____ Sand and varnish the rudder, tiller and centerboard.

_____ Rinse all lines in fresh water and coil.

_____ Remove everything removeable and take home.

_____ Get a good, strong cover for the boat and tie it securely.

_____ Go home and wait for spring!